Series 9/10
Exam Secrets
Study Guide

Dear Future Exam Success Story

First of all, **THANK YOU** for purchasing Mometrix study materials!

Second, congratulations! You are one of the few determined test-takers who are committed to doing whatever it takes to excel on your exam. **You have come to the right place.** We developed these study materials with one goal in mind: to deliver you the information you need in a format that's concise and easy to use.

In addition to optimizing your guide for the content of the test, we've outlined our recommended steps for breaking down the preparation process into small, attainable goals so you can make sure you stay on track.

We've also analyzed the entire test-taking process, identifying the most common pitfalls and showing how you can overcome them and be ready for any curveball the test throws you.

Standardized testing is one of the biggest obstacles on your road to success, which only increases the importance of doing well in the high-pressure, high-stakes environment of test day. Your results on this test could have a significant impact on your future, and this guide provides the information and practical advice to help you achieve your full potential on test day.

Your success is our success

We would love to hear from you! If you would like to share the story of your exam success or if you have any questions or comments in regard to our products, please contact us at **800-673-8175** or **support@mometrix.com**.

Thanks again for your business and we wish you continued success!

Sincerely,
The Mometrix Test Preparation Team

Need more help? Check out our flashcards at:
http://MometrixFlashcards.com/Series910

TABLE OF CONTENTS

Introduction

Thank you for purchasing this resource! You have made the choice to prepare yourself for a test that could have a huge impact on your future, and this guide is designed to help you be fully ready for test day. Obviously, it's important to have a solid understanding of the test material, but you also need to be prepared for the unique environment and stressors of the test, so that you can perform to the best of your abilities.

For this purpose, the first section that appears in this guide is the **Secret Keys**. We've devoted countless hours to meticulously researching what works and what doesn't, and we've boiled down our findings to the five most impactful steps you can take to improve your performance on the test. We start at the beginning with study planning and move through the preparation process, all the way to the testing strategies that will help you get the most out of what you know when you're finally sitting in front of the test.

We recommend that you start preparing for your test as far in advance as possible. However, if you've bought this guide as a last-minute study resource and only have a few days before your test, we recommend that you skip over the first two Secret Keys since they address a long-term study plan.

If you struggle with **test anxiety**, we strongly encourage you to check out our recommendations for how you can overcome it. Test anxiety is a formidable foe, but it can be beaten, and we want to make sure you have the tools you need to defeat it.

Secret Key 1: Plan Big, Study Small

There's a lot riding on your performance. If you want to ace this test, you're going to need to keep your skills sharp and the material fresh in your mind. You need a plan that lets you review everything you need to know while still fitting in your schedule. We'll break this strategy down into three categories.

Information Organization

Start with the information you already have: the official test outline. From this, you can make a complete list of all the concepts you need to cover before the test. Organize these concepts into groups that can be studied together, and create a list of any related vocabulary you need to learn so you can brush up on any difficult terms. You'll want to keep this vocabulary list handy once you actually start studying since you may need to add to it along the way.

Time Management

Once you have your set of study concepts, decide how to spread them out over the time you have left before the test. Break your study plan into small, clear goals so you have a manageable task for each day and know exactly what you're doing. Then just focus on one small step at a time. When you manage your time this way, you don't need to spend hours at a time studying. Studying a small block of content for a short period each day helps you retain information better and avoid stressing over how much you have left to do. You can relax knowing that you have a plan to cover everything in time. In order for this strategy to be effective though, you have to start studying early and stick to your schedule. Avoid the exhaustion and futility that comes from last-minute cramming!

Study Environment

The environment you study in has a big impact on your learning. Studying in a coffee shop, while probably more enjoyable, is not likely to be as fruitful as studying in a quiet room. It's important to keep distractions to a minimum. You're only planning to study for a short block of time, so make the most of it. Don't pause to check your phone or get up to find a snack. It's also important to **avoid multitasking**. Research has consistently shown that multitasking will make your studying dramatically less effective. Your study area should also be comfortable and well-lit so you don't have the distraction of straining your eyes or sitting on an uncomfortable chair.

The time of day you study is also important. You want to be rested and alert. Don't wait until just before bedtime. Study when you'll be most likely to comprehend and remember. Even better, if you know what time of day your test will be, set that time aside for study. That way your brain will be used to working on that subject at that specific time and you'll have a better chance of recalling information.

Finally, it can be helpful to team up with others who are studying for the same test. Your actual studying should be done in as isolated an environment as possible, but the work of organizing the information and setting up the study plan can be divided up. In between study sessions, you can discuss with your teammates the concepts that you're all studying and quiz each other on the details. Just be sure that your teammates are as serious about the test as you are. If you find that your study time is being replaced with social time, you might need to find a new team.

Secret Key 2: Make Your Studying Count

You're devoting a lot of time and effort to preparing for this test, so you want to be absolutely certain it will pay off. This means doing more than just reading the content and hoping you can remember it on test day. It's important to make every minute of study count. There are two main areas you can focus on to make your studying count.

Retention

It doesn't matter how much time you study if you can't remember the material. You need to make sure you are retaining the concepts. To check your retention of the information you're learning, try recalling it at later times with minimal prompting. Try carrying around flashcards and glance at one or two from time to time or ask a friend who's also studying for the test to quiz you.

To enhance your retention, look for ways to put the information into practice so that you can apply it rather than simply recalling it. If you're using the information in practical ways, it will be much easier to remember. Similarly, it helps to solidify a concept in your mind if you're not only reading it to yourself but also explaining it to someone else. Ask a friend to let you teach them about a concept you're a little shaky on (or speak aloud to an imaginary audience if necessary). As you try to summarize, define, give examples, and answer your friend's questions, you'll understand the concepts better and they will stay with you longer. Finally, step back for a big picture view and ask yourself how each piece of information fits with the whole subject. When you link the different concepts together and see them working together as a whole, it's easier to remember the individual components.

Finally, practice showing your work on any multi-step problems, even if you're just studying. Writing out each step you take to solve a problem will help solidify the process in your mind, and you'll be more likely to remember it during the test.

Modality

Modality simply refers to the means or method by which you study. Choosing a study modality that fits your own individual learning style is crucial. No two people learn best in exactly the same way, so it's important to know your strengths and use them to your advantage.

4

For example, if you learn best by visualization, focus on visualizing a concept in your mind and draw an image or a diagram. Try color-coding your notes, illustrating them, or creating symbols that will trigger your mind to recall a learned concept. If you learn best by hearing or discussing information, find a study partner who learns the same way or read aloud to yourself. Think about how to put the information in your own words. Imagine that you are giving a lecture on the topic and record yourself so you can listen to it later.

For any learning style, flashcards can be helpful. Organize the information so you can take advantage of spare moments to review. Underline key words or phrases. Use different colors for different categories. Mnemonic devices (such as creating a short list in which every item starts with the same letter) can also help with retention. Find what works best for you and use it to store the information in your mind most effectively and easily.

Secret Key 3: Practice the Right Way

Your success on test day depends not only on how many hours you put into preparing, but also on whether you prepared the right way. It's good to check along the way to see if your studying is paying off. One of the most effective ways to do this is by taking practice tests to evaluate your progress. Practice tests are useful because they show exactly where you need to improve. Every time you take a practice test, pay special attention to these three groups of questions:

- The questions you got wrong
- The questions you had to guess on, even if you guessed right
- The questions you found difficult or slow to work through

This will show you exactly what your weak areas are, and where you need to devote more study time. Ask yourself why each of these questions gave you trouble. Was it because you didn't understand the material? Was it because you didn't remember the vocabulary? Do you need more repetitions on this type of question to build speed and confidence? Dig into those questions and figure out how you can strengthen your weak areas as you go back to review the material.

 Additionally, many practice tests have a section explaining the answer choices. It can be tempting to read the explanation and think that you now have a good understanding of the concept. However, an explanation likely only covers part of the question's broader context. Even if the explanation makes perfect sense, **go back and investigate** every concept related to the question until you're positive you have a thorough understanding.

As you go along, keep in mind that the practice test is just that: practice. Memorizing these questions and answers will not be very helpful on the actual test because it is unlikely to have any of the same exact questions. If you only know the right answers to the sample questions, you won't be prepared for the real thing. **Study the concepts** until you understand them fully, and then you'll be able to answer any question that shows up on the test.

It's important to wait on the practice tests until you're ready. If you take a test on your first day of study, you may be overwhelmed by the amount of material covered and how much you need to learn. Work up to it gradually.

On test day, you'll need to be prepared for answering questions, managing your time, and using the test-taking strategies you've learned. It's a lot to balance, like a mental marathon that will have a big impact on your future. Like training for a marathon, you'll need to start slowly and work your way up. When test day arrives, you'll be ready.

6

Start with the strategies you've read in the first two Secret Keys—plan your course and study in the way that works best for you. If you have time, consider using multiple study resources to get different approaches to the same concepts. It can be helpful to see difficult concepts from more than one angle. Then find a good source for practice tests. Many times, the test website will suggest potential study resources or provide sample tests.

Practice Test Strategy

If you're able to find at least three practice tests, we recommend this strategy:

UNTIMED AND OPEN-BOOK PRACTICE

Take the first test with no time constraints and with your notes and study guide handy. Take your time and focus on applying the strategies you've learned.

TIMED AND OPEN-BOOK PRACTICE

Take the second practice test open-book as well, but set a timer and practice pacing yourself to finish in time.

TIMED AND CLOSED-BOOK PRACTICE

Take any other practice tests as if it were test day. Set a timer and put away your study materials. Sit at a table or desk in a quiet room, imagine yourself at the testing center, and answer questions as quickly and accurately as possible.

Keep repeating timed and closed-book tests on a regular basis until you run out of practice tests or it's time for the actual test. Your mind will be ready for the schedule and stress of test day, and you'll be able to focus on recalling the material you've learned.

Secret Key 4: Pace Yourself

Once you're fully prepared for the material on the test, your biggest challenge on test day will be managing your time. Just knowing that the clock is ticking can make you panic even if you have plenty of time left. Work on pacing yourself so you can build confidence against the time constraints of the exam. Pacing is a difficult skill to master, especially in a high-pressure environment, so **practice is vital**.

Set time expectations for your pace based on how much time is available. For example, if a section has 60 questions and the time limit is 30 minutes, you know you have to average 30 seconds or less per question in order to answer them all. Although 30 seconds is the hard limit, set 25 seconds per question as your goal, so you reserve extra time to spend on harder questions. When you budget extra time for the harder questions, you no longer have any reason to stress when those questions take longer to answer.

Don't let this time expectation distract you from working through the test at a calm, steady pace, but keep it in mind so you don't spend too much time on any one question. Recognize that taking extra time on one question you don't understand may keep you from answering two that you do understand later in the test. If your time limit for a question is up and you're still not sure of the answer, mark it and move on, and come back to it later if the time and the test format allow. If the testing format doesn't allow you to return to earlier questions, just make an educated guess; then put it out of your mind and move on.

On the easier questions, be careful not to rush. It may seem wise to hurry through them so you have more time for the challenging ones, but it's not worth missing one if you know the concept and just didn't take the time to read the question fully. Work efficiently but make sure you understand the question and have looked at all of the answer choices, since more than one may seem right at first.

Even if you're paying attention to the time, you may find yourself a little behind at some point. You should speed up to get back on track, but do so wisely. Don't panic; just take a few seconds less on each question until you're caught up. Don't guess without thinking, but do look through the answer choices and eliminate any you know are wrong. If you can get down to two choices, it is often worthwhile to guess from those. Once you've chosen an answer, move on and don't dwell on any that you skipped or had to hurry through. If a question was taking too long, chances are it was one of the harder ones, so you weren't as likely to get it right anyway.

On the other hand, if you find yourself getting ahead of schedule, it may be beneficial to slow down a little. The more quickly you work, the more likely you are to make a careless mistake that will affect your score. You've budgeted time for each question, so don't be afraid to spend that time. Practice an efficient but careful pace to get the most out of the time you have.

Secret Key 5: Have a Plan for Guessing

When you're taking the test, you may find yourself stuck on a question. Some of the answer choices seem better than others, but you don't see the one answer choice that is obviously correct. What do you do?

The scenario described above is very common, yet most test takers have not effectively prepared for it. Developing and practicing a plan for guessing may be one of the single most effective uses of your time as you get ready for the exam.

In developing your plan for guessing, there are three questions to address:

- When should you start the guessing process?
- How should you narrow down the choices?
- Which answer should you choose?

When to Start the Guessing Process

Unless your plan for guessing is to select C every time (which, despite its merits, is not what we recommend), you need to leave yourself enough time to apply your answer elimination strategies. Since you have a limited amount of time for each question, that means that if you're going to give yourself the best shot at guessing correctly, you have to decide quickly whether or not you will guess.

Of course, the best-case scenario is that you don't have to guess at all, so first, see if you can answer the question based on your knowledge of the subject and basic reasoning skills. Focus on the key words in the question and try to jog your memory of related topics. Give yourself a chance to bring the knowledge to mind, but once you realize that you don't have (or you can't access) the knowledge you need to answer the question, it's time to start the guessing process.

It's almost always better to start the guessing process too early than too late. It only takes a few seconds to remember something and answer the question from knowledge. Carefully eliminating wrong answer choices takes longer. Plus, going through the process of eliminating answer choices can actually help jog your memory.

Summary: Start the guessing process as soon as you decide that you can't answer the question based on your knowledge.

10

How to Narrow Down the Choices

The next chapter in this book (**Test-Taking Strategies**) includes a wide range of strategies for how to approach questions and how to look for answer choices to eliminate. You will definitely want to read those carefully, practice them, and figure out which ones work best for you. Here though, we're going to address a mindset rather than a particular strategy.

Your odds of guessing an answer correctly depend on how many options you are choosing from.

Number of options left	5	4	3	2	1
Odds of guessing correctly	20%	25%	33%	50%	100%

You can see from this chart just how valuable it is to be able to eliminate incorrect answers and make an educated guess, but there are two things that many test takers do that cause them to miss out on the benefits of guessing:

- Accidentally eliminating the correct answer
- Selecting an answer based on an impression

We'll look at the first one here, and the second one in the next section.

To avoid accidentally eliminating the correct answer, we recommend a thought exercise called **the $5 challenge**. In this challenge, you only eliminate an answer choice from contention if you are willing to bet $5 on it being wrong. Why $5? Five dollars is a small but not insignificant amount of money. It's an amount you could

afford to lose but wouldn't want to throw away. And while losing $5 once might not hurt too much, doing it twenty times will set you back $100. In the same way, each small decision you make—eliminating a choice here, guessing on a question there—won't by itself impact your score very much, but when you put them all together, they can make a big difference. By holding each answer choice elimination decision to a higher standard, you can reduce the risk of accidentally eliminating the correct answer.

The $5 challenge can also be applied in a positive sense: If you are willing to bet $5 that an answer choice *is* correct, go ahead and mark it as correct.

Summary: Only eliminate an answer choice if you are willing to bet $5 that it is wrong.

Which Answer to Choose

You're taking the test. You've run into a hard question and decided you'll have to guess. You've eliminated all the answer choices you're willing to bet $5 on. Now you have to pick an answer. Why do we even need to talk about this? Why can't you just pick whichever one you feel like when the time comes?

The answer to these questions is that if you don't come into the test with a plan, you'll rely on your impression to select an answer choice, and if you do that, you risk falling into a trap. The test writers know that everyone who takes their test will be guessing on some of the questions, so they intentionally write wrong answer choices to seem plausible. You still have to pick an answer though, and if the wrong answer choices are designed to look right, how can you ever be sure that you're not falling for their trap? The best solution we've found to this dilemma is to take the decision out of your hands entirely. Here is the process we recommend:

Once you've eliminated any choices that you are confident (willing to bet $5) are wrong, select the first remaining choice as your answer.

Whether you choose to select the first remaining choice, the second, or the last, the important thing is that you use some preselected standard. Using this approach guarantees that you will not be enticed into selecting an answer choice that looks right, because you are not basing your decision on how the answer choices look.

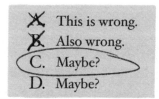

This is not meant to make you question your knowledge. Instead, it is to help you recognize the difference between your knowledge and your impressions. There's a huge difference between thinking an answer is right because of what you know, and thinking an answer is right because it looks or sounds like it should be right.

Summary: To ensure that your selection is appropriately random, make a predetermined selection from among all answer choices you have not eliminated.

Test-Taking Strategies

This section contains a list of test-taking strategies that you may find helpful as you work through the test. By taking what you know and applying logical thought, you can maximize your chances of answering any question correctly!

It is very important to realize that every question is different and every person is different: no single strategy will work on every question, and no single strategy will work for every person. That's why we've included all of them here, so you can try them out and determine which ones work best for different types of questions and which ones work best for you.

Question Strategies

⊘ READ CAREFULLY

Read the question and the answer choices carefully. Don't miss the question because you misread the terms. You have plenty of time to read each question thoroughly and make sure you understand what is being asked. Yet a happy medium must be attained, so don't waste too much time. You must read carefully and efficiently.

⊘ CONTEXTUAL CLUES

Look for contextual clues. If the question includes a word you are not familiar with, look at the immediate context for some indication of what the word might mean. Contextual clues can often give you all the information you need to decipher the meaning of an unfamiliar word. Even if you can't determine the meaning, you may be able to narrow down the possibilities enough to make a solid guess at the answer to the question.

⊘ PREFIXES

If you're having trouble with a word in the question or answer choices, try dissecting it. Take advantage of every clue that the word might include. Prefixes can be a huge help. Usually, they allow you to determine a basic meaning. *Pre-* means before, *post-* means after, *pro-* is positive, *de-* is negative. From prefixes, you can get an idea of the general meaning of the word and try to put it into context.

⊘ HEDGE WORDS

Watch out for critical hedge words, such as *likely, may, can, sometimes, often, almost, mostly, usually, generally, rarely,* and *sometimes.* Question writers insert these hedge phrases to cover every possibility. Often an answer choice will be wrong simply because it leaves no room for exception. Be on guard for answer choices that have definitive words such as *exactly* and *always.*

13

⏱ Switchback Words

Stay alert for *switchbacks*. These are the words and phrases frequently used to alert you to shifts in thought. The most common switchback words are *but*, *although*, and *however*. Others include *nevertheless*, *on the other hand*, *even though*, *while*, *in spite of*, *despite*, and *regardless of*. Switchback words are important to catch because they can change the direction of the question or an answer choice.

⏱ Face Value

When in doubt, use common sense. Accept the situation in the problem at face value. Don't read too much into it. These problems will not require you to make wild assumptions. If you have to go beyond creativity and warp time or space in order to have an answer choice fit the question, then you should move on and consider the other answer choices. These are normal problems rooted in reality. The applicable relationship or explanation may not be readily apparent, but it is there for you to figure out. Use your common sense to interpret anything that isn't clear.

Answer Choice Strategies

⏱ Answer Selection

The most thorough way to pick an answer choice is to identify and eliminate wrong answers until only one is left, then confirm it is the correct answer. Sometimes an answer choice may immediately seem right, but be careful. The test writers will usually put more than one reasonable answer choice on each question, so take a second to read all of them and make sure that the other choices are not equally obvious. As long as you have time left, it is better to read every answer choice than to pick the first one that looks right without checking the others.

⏱ Answer Choice Families

An answer choice family consists of two (in rare cases, three) answer choices that are very similar in construction and cannot all be true at the same time. If you see two answer choices that are direct opposites or parallels, one of them is usually the correct answer. For instance, if one answer choice says that quantity x increases and another either says that quantity x decreases (opposite) or says that quantity y increases (parallel), then those answer choices would fall into the same family. An answer choice that doesn't match the construction of the answer choice family is more likely to be incorrect. Most questions will not have answer choice families, but when they do appear, you should be prepared to recognize them.

⏱ Eliminate Answers

Eliminate answer choices as soon as you realize they are wrong, but make sure you consider all possibilities. If you are eliminating answer choices and realize that the last one you are left with is also wrong, don't panic. Start over and consider each choice again. There may be something you missed the first time that you will realize on the second pass.

14

⊘ AVOID FACT TRAPS

Don't be distracted by an answer choice that is factually true but doesn't answer the question. You are looking for the choice that answers the question. Stay focused on what the question is asking for so you don't accidentally pick an answer that is true but incorrect. Always go back to the question and make sure the answer choice you've selected actually answers the question and is not merely a true statement.

⊘ EXTREME STATEMENTS

In general, you should avoid answers that put forth extreme actions as standard practice or proclaim controversial ideas as established fact. An answer choice that states the "process should be used in certain situations, if..." is much more likely to be correct than one that states the "process should be discontinued completely." The first is a calm rational statement and doesn't even make a definitive, uncompromising stance, using a hedge word *if* to provide wiggle room, whereas the second choice is far more extreme.

⊘ BENCHMARK

As you read through the answer choices and you come across one that seems to answer the question well, mentally select that answer choice. This is not your final answer, but it's the one that will help you evaluate the other answer choices. The one that you selected is your benchmark or standard for judging each of the other answer choices. Every other answer choice must be compared to your benchmark. That choice is correct until proven otherwise by another answer choice beating it. If you find a better answer, then that one becomes your new benchmark. Once you've decided that no other choice answers the question as well as your benchmark, you have your final answer.

⊘ PREDICT THE ANSWER

Before you even start looking at the answer choices, it is often best to try to predict the answer. When you come up with the answer on your own, it is easier to avoid distractions and traps because you will know exactly what to look for. The right answer choice is unlikely to be word-for-word what you came up with, but it should be a close match. Even if you are confident that you have the right answer, you should still take the time to read each option before moving on.

General Strategies

⊘ TOUGH QUESTIONS

If you are stumped on a problem or it appears too hard or too difficult, don't waste time. Move on! Remember though, if you can quickly check for obviously incorrect answer choices, your chances of guessing correctly are greatly improved. Before you completely give up, at least try to knock out a couple of possible answers. Eliminate what you can and then guess at the remaining answer choices before moving on.

15

⊘ Check Your Work

Since you will probably not know every term listed and the answer to every question, it is important that you get credit for the ones that you do know. Don't miss any questions through careless mistakes. If at all possible, try to take a second to look back over your answer selection and make sure you've selected the correct answer choice and haven't made a costly careless mistake (such as marking an answer choice that you didn't mean to mark). This quick double check should more than pay for itself in caught mistakes for the time it costs.

⊘ Pace Yourself

It's easy to be overwhelmed when you're looking at a page full of questions; your mind is confused and full of random thoughts, and the clock is ticking down faster than you would like. Calm down and maintain the pace that you have set for yourself. Especially as you get down to the last few minutes of the test, don't let the small numbers on the clock make you panic. As long as you are on track by monitoring your pace, you are guaranteed to have time for each question.

⊘ Don't Rush

It is very easy to make errors when you are in a hurry. Maintaining a fast pace in answering questions is pointless if it makes you miss questions that you would have gotten right otherwise. Test writers like to include distracting information and wrong answers that seem right. Taking a little extra time to avoid careless mistakes can make all the difference in your test score. Find a pace that allows you to be confident in the answers that you select.

⊘ Keep Moving

Panicking will not help you pass the test, so do your best to stay calm and keep moving. Taking deep breaths and going through the answer elimination steps you practiced can help to break through a stress barrier and keep your pace.

Final Notes

The combination of a solid foundation of content knowledge and the confidence that comes from practicing your plan for applying that knowledge is the key to maximizing your performance on test day. As your foundation of content knowledge is built up and strengthened, you'll find that the strategies included in this chapter become more and more effective in helping you quickly sift through the distractions and traps of the test to isolate the correct answer.

Now that you're preparing to move forward into the test content chapters of this book, be sure to keep your goal in mind. As you read, think about how you will be able to apply this information on the test. If you've already seen sample questions for the test and you have an idea of the question format and style, try to come up with questions of your own that you can answer based on what you're reading. This will give you valuable practice applying your knowledge in the same ways you can expect to on test day.

Good luck and good studying!

Series 10

Supervise Associated Persons and Personnel Management Activities

BACKGROUND CHECKS

Before a registered principal approves the hire of a new individual, he must submit the individual to a rigorous background check. This background check can include many different sources. Credit checks are often performed to ensure that the applicant does not have an onerous credit rating, which may indicate a higher likelihood to embezzle client funds. Criminal background checks are useful for ensuring that the firm is not hiring an individual who may not be eligible to work for them, or who has committed previous financial crimes. If the potential hire has been previously associated with another FINRA firm, the principal should also investigate their Form U-4 to verify that they don't have current injunctions or prior convictions that may preclude them from employment.

FORM U-4

Form U-4 is a form that must be registered with FINRA which contains the applicant's personal information such as name, address, date of birth, tax identification number, address of residence for the preceding five years, employment history for the preceding 10 years, any bankruptcies suffered, aliases under which the person may have operated, whether a fidelity bond was denied to the individual, whether the applicant has had convictions involving securities in the prior 10 years, disciplinary actions taken by the applicable self-regulatory organization (SRO), and if the applicant is the recipient of an injunction. All registered broker/dealers must file a Form U-4. Additionally, all parties that work either on behalf of or for the broker/dealer must maintain a current Form U-4. It is the responsibility of the registered principal to ensure that all U-4 forms are updated with the most current information to guarantee compliance with their SRO.

DISQUALIFICATIONS FOR REGISTRATION WITH FINRA

FINRA has identified several events that immediately disqualify an individual from registration with the organization. If an individual has knowingly and intentionally broken securities law; has had his or her registration revoked or suspended by another regulatory body; caused a suspension or revocation of registration; been associated with individuals causing suspension or revocation of registration; falsified information filed with another regulatory body; is subject to a ruling by the Securities and Exchange Commission forbidding his or her registration; has been restricted from transacting securities by a civil judge; or has, within the past 10 years, been convicted of a misdemeanor involving financial transaction, or a felony in general, then FINRA will not approve the registrant's application.

19

FINGERPRINTING REQUIREMENTS

Any member of a national securities exchange, broker, dealer, registered transfer agent or registered clearing agency must require each of its partners, directors, officers, and employees be fingerprinted and submit the fingerprints to the Attorney General of the United States, with some exemptions.

CONTINUING EDUCATION REQUIREMENTS FOR MEMBERSHIP AND REGISTRATION

Continuing education is required for certain registered people after they have passed their initial qualifying examinations. The purpose of the continuing education is to make certain that the member is kept up-to-date with changes to rules and quiz the member on ethical standards. The continuing education requirements consist of a regulatory element and a firm element. The regulatory element is performed by the Financial Industry Regulatory Authority (FINRA). Once a member has held his or her registration for a period of 2 years, they must participate in regulatory training. From that point on, it is required every 3 years. The individual has 120 days to complete the training (from the due date) or else the registration will be made inactive until the training is completed. The firm element is a continuing education program administered by the member firm. It is required to be delivered to all locations where people are registered and must touch on the topics of general investment features and their associated risk factors, suitability and sales practice considerations, applicable regulatory requirements, and training on ethics.

REGULATORY ELEMENT

Members are to meet the continuing education requirements, their regulatory element, on their 2nd registration anniversary and every three years thereafter. If it is not completed, the person's registration will be deemed inactive. A registered person is required to retake the regulatory element and satisfy all the requirements if the person is subject to a statutory disqualification, is subject to a suspension, or is ordered to as part of a sanction. If FINRA procedures are followed, a firm can have an "in-firm" administration of the regulatory requirement for their registered persons.

FIRM ELEMENT

A member firm must maintain a continuing and current education program for its covered registered persons to enhance the securities skills, knowledge, and professionalism. Annually, a member is to evaluate and prioritize his training needs and develop a plan.

FINRA RULE 4530

Under FINRA Rule 4530, FINRA member firms should report violations within 30 calendar days of their occurrence. Part B of Rule 4530 allows the member time to determine that an actual violation has occurred and specifies the firm "to report to FINRA within 30 calendar days after the firm has concluded, or reasonably should have concluded, on its own that the firm or an associated person of the firm has violated any securities, insurance, commodities, financial or investment-related laws, rules, regulations or standards of conduct of any domestic or foreign regulatory body or self-regulatory organization." Rule 4530 further goes on to state that customer "statistical and summary information" regarding customer complaints should be filed each quarter by the 15th calendar day following the end of the quarter. Some FINRA members create their own reporting guidelines, but these guidelines must always be at least as frequent as those outlined in Rule 4530. Many members set up stricter reporting guidelines. Following stricter reporting dates will help prevent the registered person from violating FINRA rules.

REPORTING REQUIREMENTS

A member is required to report it within 30 calendar days if the member or an associated person:

- has violated any governing laws, rules, regulations, or standards of conduct
- is the subject of any written consumer complaint involving theft, misappropriation of funds or securities, or forgery
- is named as a defendant in a proceeding alleging violation of the Exchange Act of other governing legislature
- is denied registration or is expelled or otherwise disciplined by a regulatory body
- is indicted, convicted, or pleads guilty to any felony, or misdemeanor involving the purchase or sale of securities, taking of false oath, theft, larceny, robbery, and other pertinent misdemeanors
- is a director, controlling stockholder, or certain other officers of a broker, dealer, or investment company that was suspended, expelled, or had its registration denied or revoked
- is a defendant in certain securities, commodities, or financial related litigations
- is engaged in certain business transactions with a person that is statutorily disqualified as defined in the Exchange Act
- is subject to certain disciplinary action

A member is to report, information regarding written customer complaints by the fifteenth day of the month after it was received.

NASD MEMBERSHIP APPLICATION PROCESS

Pursuant to NASD Rule 1013, the new member application shall consist of the following information:

- Form NMA
- An original signed and notarized paper Form BD
- An original FINRA-approved fingerprint card for each associated person
- A new member assessment report

- A detailed business plan, including financial statements, organizational chart, locations of businesses, types of securities to be offered, description of sales practices, description of business facilities and copies of any lease or purchase agreements, and any other such information that may impact financial performance over the following 12 months
- A description of any recent civil or criminal proceedings
- A description of the record-keeping system to be utilized
- A description of the supervisory system and procedures to be utilized
- A description of the experience and qualifications of supervisors and registered principals
- An agreement to abide by Firm Element continuing education requirements

ENSURING REPRESENTATIVES ARE REGISTERED

A registered representative must be registered with the administrator in any state in which the representative transacts business. This includes any state in which the representative represents clients. The registration process required varies by state, but they tend to be very similar. Once registered representatives pass the requisite FINRA exam, they usually need only pay the licensing fee to the state administrator's office. This fee is to offset record keeping costs associated with maintaining a representative's records with the state.

It is the responsibility of the supervisor to ensure that all representatives under his or her supervision are appropriately registered in all states in which they do business. This is generally accomplished through automatically generated reports that will inform the supervisor if the representative has new business in a state other than one in which they are registered to transact.

FINRA CONTINUING EDUCATION REQUIREMENTS

As required by FINRA, registered individuals must take continuing education classes after two years of registration, and every three years after that. These continuing education classes must be approved by FINRA specifically for the reason of meeting the continuing education requirement, and administered by a proctor who FINRA has approved for the purpose of administering the continuing education. If a representative fails to complete the requirement, he may lose his FINRA registration. The supervising registered principal may assist the registered representative in this matter, and should consider it his or her responsibility to ensure that all registered representatives under their supervision are aware of the continuing education requirement and the time frame in which they must complete that requirement. In addition to the FINRA continuing education, or the regulatory element, the registered individual must also complete the firm element of the continuing education. The firm element is typically computer-based training established by the FINRA member and administered to all registered employees on a yearly basis.

ASSOCIATED PERSONS AND INDEPENDENT CONTRACTORS

Persons considered associated with FINRA members (usually broker/dealers) are any that are under the control of the broker/dealer or who may be responsible in some capacity for the operation of the broker/dealer. While this definition includes officers of the firm and registered representatives that the firm has sponsored, it specifically excludes clerical staff members that do not execute securities-related business. Independent contractors are those individuals that are hired by the FINRA member to perform a specific task, such as research, on an individual basis. While independent contractors may be hired for multiple projects, their employment is not considered continuous. The registered principal (RP) is responsible for ensuring that persons associated with the FINRA member are compliant with all regulations and rules set forth by their SRO. However, they are not responsible for the compliance of the independent contractor. While the RP must ensure that the firm is compliant when hiring an independent contractor, it is the responsibility of the contractor's firm to ensure their compliance.

OFFICE OF SUPERVISORY JURISDICTION

FINRA requires each of its members to designate certain offices within the organization as offices of supervisory jurisdiction, or OSJs. OSJs are defined as any office in which a combination of the following occur: order execution or market making, supervision of outlying offices, custody of assets is received, approval of advertising is given, creation of public or private offerings, new account approval, and approval of client orders. Offices of supervisory jurisdiction must have at least one registered principal on staff. OSJs are responsible for ensuring that the firm's written supervision guidelines are followed, reviewing client accounts, inspecting outlying offices for which they are responsible, and maintaining client records

BRANCH OFFICES

According to Rule 3010 of the NASD (now superseded by FINRA), any place where a member of a FINRA firm regularly transacts securities business is considered a branch office. Such a general statement could lead to many restaurants and hotels being considered branch offices, so Rule 3010 specifically excludes certain locations from the definition of branch office. Excluded from Rule 3010's definition of branch office are firm offices where securities are not transacted, transitory locations of offices that the firm is required to use due to the business continuity plan, trading floors, the non-business home address of an associated person, any place that is used less than 30 days a year for business, office locations specifically not used for securities business (must transact less than 25 securities transactions per year), and any location that is used primarily for its convenience but is not used regularly (i.e., obtaining transactional approval from a client over a lunch meeting).

MARGIN REQUIREMENT TERMS

The following are terms as found in FINRA Rule 4210 regarding margin requirements:

Basket — a group of stocks eligible to be executed in a single trade.

Designated account — an account of certain banks, investment companies, insurance companies, state or political subdivisions, or pension plans.

Margin — the necessary amount of equity to be maintained for a security position in an account.

Major foreign sovereign debt — a debt security issued by a foreign entity that has debt securities that are subordinated in relation and the security has been ranked in the top rating category by a nationally recognized rating organization.

Exempt account — any member or registered broker-dealer, or certain persons with a net worth of $45 million or more.

Other marginable non-equity securities — include certain debt securities that are not traded on a national exchange and certain private pass-through securities.

INITIAL MARGIN AND MAINTENANCE MARGIN

As outlined in FINRA Rule 4210, the initial margin and maintenance margin are:

- Initial margin - the required opening deposit in a margin account.
- Maintenance margin - the required margin which must be maintained in an account, calculated as:
  - 25% of the current market value of securities
  - the greater of $2.50 per share or 100% of the current market value for any stock short positions of stock trading at less than $5 per share
  - the greater of $5 per share or 100% of the current market value for any stock short positions of stock trading at more than $5 per share
  - the greater of $5 per share or 30% of the current market value for each bond short position
  - 20% of the current market value for any security futures contracts
  - 100% of the current market value for non-margin eligible securities held "long"

THIRD-PARTY TRADING AUTHORIZATION AND DISCRETIONARY AUTHORITY

Third-party trading authorization describes authority to transact given to someone other than the account owner. This often takes the form of a person given power of attorney to transact for another party. Limited third-party authorization gives the third party the authority only to transact securities in their account. Full third-party trading authorization empowers the third party to transact in and request distributions from the account. Distributions requested by fully authorized third parties must still be payable to the account owner. Discretionary trading authority refers to authority that the account owner gives a registered individual to transact in their account without their prior consent. Trading may also be considered discretionary if the client asks the registered person to determine a particular portion of the trade. These facets of the trades are often referred to as the three A's: action, asset, and amount. If the adviser determines any of the preceding three aspects without prior client consent, he must have discretionary authority on the

24

Copyright © Mometrix Media. You have been licensed one copy of this document for personal use only. Any other reproduction or redistribution is strictly prohibited. All rights reserved. This content is provided for test preparation purposes only and does not imply an endorsement by Mometrix of any particular political, scientific, or religious point of view.

account. Discretionary authority must be given in writing and approved by a registered principal.

NASD RULE 3050

NASD Rule 3050 regarding transactions for or by associated persons is explained below:

- Determine adverse interest - a member who knowingly executes a transaction to purchase or sell a security for the account of person associated with another member is to use due diligence in ensuring that the transaction will not adversely affect the persons employing member.
- Obligations of executing member - the executing member is to notify the employing member in writing prior to execution; to transmit copies of confirmations, statements, or other information upon request; and to notify the person associated of the intent to provide such information.
- Obligations of associated persons concerning an account with a member - the person associated in such a transaction is to notify both the executing member and employing member of his association with each.
- Obligations of associated persons concerning an account with an investment adviser, bank, or other financial institution - if a person associated with a member opens a securities account or places an order for the purchase or sale of a security with a notice-registered broker or dealer, investment advisor, bank, or other financial institution that is not a member, the person is to notify his employing member in writing and, upon the written request of the employing member, request in writing that the financial institution provides the employing member with copies of confirmations, statements, or other financial information.
- Exemption for transactions in investment company shares and unit investment trusts - the Rule is not applicable to transactions in certain unit investment trusts and variable contracts or redeemable securities.

FINRA RULE 3220

FINRA established Rule 3220 to regulate the "influence or rewarding employees of others." The most common form of this influence comes in the form of gifts from investment companies (usually via their wholesalers) to registered individuals. Rule 3220 states that registered representatives (RRs) may not accept more than $100 per year from another FINRA member, or from customers (or give gifts of greater than $100 in value to customers). Records of gifts given or received must be saved for three years, and made available to regulators at their request. Under no circumstances may a FINRA member give any consideration (cash or valuable items) to induce a publisher to publish information that may change the value of a security. Rule 3220 is not usually applied to sales contests or tokens commemorating business transactions between FINRA members, even when the value of the token exceeds $100.

FINRA RULE 3270

FINRA established Rule 3270 to prevent employees of FINRA members from being subject to conflicts of interest that may arise from dual employment. For example, a registered representative (RR) of a well-regarded FINRA member may present an investment not actually associated with their FINRA member employer, and the buyer may associate the stability of the investment with the FINRA member's reputation. To prevent situations like this, FINRA Rule 3270 requires that before member employees accept outside employment, they must first receive permission from their employer, and disclose in a timely fashion any changes or additional employment taken. FINRA Rule 3270 does not apply to passive income because the employee cannot affect truly passive income activities. Before the activity is approved, it is the job of the registered principal to determine if it will "interfere with or otherwise compromise the registered person's responsibilities to the member and/or the member's customers or be viewed by customers or the public as part of the member's business based upon, among other factors, the nature of the proposed activity and the manner in which it will be offered."

FINRA RULE 5110

The following are components of FINRA Rule 5110:

- Underwriting compensation and arrangements - all underwriting terms and agreements have to be fair and reasonable. All compensation in relation to underwriting a security has to be fair and reasonable.
- Items included in compensation - all items of value received or that will be received by an underwriter in connection with a distribution starting from 180 days before the filing date are considered to be compensation and have to be disclosed in the prospectus.
- Valuation of non-cash compensation - a security cannot be received by an underwriter as compensation in connection with a public offering unless the security is identical to the security issued to the public or the security can be accurately valued. Calculated compensation value is usually in some way based on, or derived from, the market price or public offering price.
- Non-cash compensation - is restricted, and includes small gifts, occasional meals, and entertainment events.

REGISTERED INDIVIDUALS HOLDING ACCOUNTS AT OTHER MEMBERS' FIRMS

In the event that an employee of a FINRA member wishes to open an investment account (whether with qualified or non-qualified funds) with another FINRA member, he must receive prior approval from his employing FINRA member. This requirement is in place to ensure that FINRA-member registered employees are not violating their own firm's rules at another firm, and also to help catch and prevent selling away. While FINRA member employees are allowed to open investment accounts with other FINRA members, they must submit to their firm's approval procedures. It is the duty of the registered principal (RP) to review an employee's request and determine whether or not the employee should be allowed to open the account. Many FINRA members disallow holding outside accounts altogether, while some only allow outside accounts with members with whom they already have a business relationship. In the event that the account is approved by an RP, the employee must have duplicate statements and confirmations sent to his employing firm so that the RP may be able to monitor the employee's actions for illegal activity.

CUSTOMERS ACCORDING TO MSRB

The Municipal Securities Rulemaking Board, or MSRB, defines the term "customer" differently than other self-regulatory organizations (SRO). Generally, the MSRB defines a customer as any legal person except a broker/dealer that is dealing in municipal securities, or an issuer of municipal securities. There are exceptions to this generalization. Firms that are trading with a municipal securities firm in a principal capacity are not considered customers; however, if they are trading in an agency capacity, they are considered customers. The MSRB assigns the term "customer" to those who may need protection due to lack of knowledge and/or experience investing in the municipal market; by definition, this excludes those who have intimate knowledge of municipal securities such as directors of municipal security firms.

MUNICIPAL FUND SECURITIES

Municipal fund securities behave similarly to mutual funds, but they are issued and administered by a municipality and benefit from the registration exemption from which municipal securities benefit. To further differentiate from mutual funds, the issuing municipality does not have to provide a prospectus, calculate the net asset value (NAV) daily, or establish a board of directors. While they are exempt from the preceding requirements, municipal funds are subject to the rules of the Municipal Securities Rulemaking Board (MSRB). While municipal bonds and municipal funds share a common issuer, they differ in that municipal funds are not fixed income instruments, and do not issue regular coupons. Municipal funds are issued in two varieties: local government investment pools (LGIP) and 529 college savings plans.

MUNICIPAL INVESTMENT FUND LOCAL GOVERNMENT INVESTMENT POOLS

Local government investment pools, or LGIPs, are municipal funds that are established by state governments to facilitate the investment of public money of smaller local governments that is not currently being used for designated projects. While state governments are free to administer LGIPs as they see fit, they usually contract experienced investment companies for LGIP management. Typically, municipalities invest directly in LGIPs, as they are not required to use a broker/dealer, and the issuers are not subject to the rules of the Municipal Securities Rulemaking Board. Because LGIPs are mostly funded with tax dollars of local municipalities, they must not carry high risk, be highly liquid, or offer yields that are competitive with comparable investments. These requirements lead to LGIPs being comprised mostly of short-term securities that are highly rated, including money market funds and US Treasury securities.

REQUIREMENTS TO LEGALLY SELL MUNICIPAL SECURITIES

Municipal securities representatives perform a multitude of functions associated with selling municipal securities. These functions all require registration of the individual (Exam Series 6 for representatives selling municipal funds, and Series 7 or 52 for all other activities) and include sales of municipal funds; direct or indirect communication with the public concerning transacting in municipal securities; the offering of investment advice regarding municipal securities; consultation for municipal securities issuers; and the underwriting, trading, and/or selling of municipal issue securities. After the individual has completed the prerequisite exam and registered with the appropriate authorities, they must complete a 90-day apprenticeship during which time they may not sell or be compensated for the sale of municipal securities. If the apprentice has previously undergone a general securities apprenticeship, this period is waived.

MSRB'S REQUIRED INFORMATION AND DISCLOSURES ON CONFIRMATIONS CONCERNING MUNICIPAL FUND TRANSACTIONS

When the broker/dealer acts in an agency capacity, the confirmation must include the other person involved in the transaction, the source of the securities, and commissions and/or other consideration given for services performed. When the broker/dealer is selling from his own inventory, he does not need to provide information regarding the markup/markdown. For both agency and principal transactions, the confirmation must include the "dated date" (if any), the date interest payments are scheduled to begin, the registration of the securities transacted, whether the securities have a call function and that call's maturity date, whether the bonds are federal taxable or contribute to any investor's alternative minimum tax considerations, the name of bond guarantor (if any), any conflicts of interest, any put options on the bond, the yield of the bond, whether the issue is in default, and whether or not the bond is unrated.

MSRB RULE G-37

The Municipal Securities Rulemaking Board (MSRB) established Rule G-37 to prevent underwriters trying to win the business of municipal securities issuers from effectively buying their business through political contributions. Political contributions are not an issue when the underwriting firm is decided through a competitive bid. In that case, the issuer simply selects the underwriter that will charge the firm the least of all the bidders. Rule G-37 takes effect through negotiated underwritings. In negotiated underwritings, a municipal securities issuer will select an underwriter and negotiate costs. Rule G-37 prevents underwriters from making political contributions to politicians who may be associated with municipal securities issuers because the politicians may direct business only to firms that make contributions to their campaign.

In order to prevent underwriters buying favorable status in municipal securities issues, MSRB Rule G-37 outlines prohibitions on municipal securities issuers doing business with underwriting firms that may have recently made political contributions to an official of the municipal securities issuer. If an official of a municipal securities underwriting firm has made a campaign contribution to an individual that may be able to affect which underwriter receives the issuer's business, then that underwriter is prohibited from transacting business with municipal securities issuers for two years. This rule includes contributions made through political actions committees (PACs) if those PACs are headed by municipal finance professionals. If the municipal finance professional is a constituent of the politician to whom he or she made a contribution, and the contribution is of $250 or less, then he or she is exempt from this rule.

NASD RULE 1070

Qualification examinations and waiver of requirements (NASD Rule 1070) - Qualification Examinations are a series of questions based on topic outlines from the Association. Results from such examinations are given to the member firms. In certain cases, NASD may waive the requirement of a Qualification Examination in lieu of other standard acceptable as proof of qualification. If a person fails the examination, he may take it again after 30 days, unless he has failed three times, in which case he must wait a period of 180 days.

NASD RULE 1080

Confidentiality of examinations (NASD Rule 1080) - the Qualification Examinations are confidential. An exam is not to be removed from the examination center, and any reproduction, disclosure, or receipt of any portion of the exam is prohibited.

DISCIPLINARY PROCEEDINGS ACCORDING TO ARTICLE XII OF FINRA'S BYLAWS

If a FINRA board of inquiry determines that a registered representative (RR) has violated a rule or law, FINRA must abide by Article XII of their by-laws in the prosecution of the accused party. According to Article XII, the accused has the right to a hearing in which he is entitled to have his side of the case heard, and may present any relevant material to sway the opinion of the determinants. In the hearing, specific charges must be brought, the RR must have an opportunity to defend against the charges, records of the hearing must be kept, and a determination must be given. The determination must include the violating act, the rules and/or regulations that the act violated, the reasoning behind the findings, and the sanctions imposed upon the RR due to the findings.

ARBITRATION OF DISPUTES BETWEEN CUSTOMERS AND MEMBERS

Arbitration is a means by which disputes are settled between two or more FINRA members, between FINRA members and customers, a FINRA member and clearing agency, a FINRA member and associated person, and between two associated persons. Arbitrations are similar to court proceedings, except that the matter is settled by an arbiter or a panel of arbiters instead of a judge. The proceedings are initiated by the claimant filing a statement of claim, documents and evidence are presented, and judgment is rendered. However, arbitration is more binding and appeals are rarely granted. It is also more difficult for one of the parties to the arbitration to request documents used in the arbitration. FINRA prefers for intra-member disputes, and customer/member disputes to be settled via arbitration

because arbitration is typically less time-consuming and more cost effective for all parties involved.

DISPUTE SETTLEMENTS SETTLED IN ARBITRATION VS. MEDIATION

Mediation is a means of conflict resolution whereby both parties agree to meet with a mediator. During the mediation, the mediator hears both sides of the dispute and offers a resolution to the dispute. If both parties accept, they may carry out the mediator's instructions and forego arbitration. If one of the parties does not accept the mediator's resolution, the case continues to arbitration. Resolutions of mediation are not binding. Arbitration, like mediation, is a form of dispute resolution in which a third party renders a decision, but the disputing parties must submit to the result of arbitration regardless of their acceptance. Additionally, arbitration results are binding, and the case may not be taken further than arbitration.

SANCTIONS IMPOSED FOR VIOLATIONS OF RULES AND REGULATIONS

When individuals register with FINRA, they agree to abide by a certain code of conduct. If that code is violated, FINRA reserves the right to sanction the individual in any combination of the following manners. FINRA may publicly censure the individual, decrying his or her activity. This can be detrimental to the individual's standing in the community and future business prospects. FINRA may also fine an individual, with the fine being proportionate to the violation committed. In a broad statement, FINRA also reserves the right to impose "any other fitting sanction." Members and their employees may be barred from association with other members, and may be suspended or have their registration suspended for a set time period. Lastly, FINRA may completely cancel membership and/or registration and forbid re-registration.

SECTION 4 OF FINRA BY-LAW ARTICLE V

Section 4 of FINRA By-Law Article V establishes a basis for which FINRA has jurisdiction regarding complaints over registered persons (or an unregistered associate of a FINRA member) for a period of time after they discontinue their registration. This is referred to as retention of jurisdiction. Generally, the period during which they remain under FINRA jurisdiction is two years. It varies slightly for registered individuals by situation. For unregistered persons associated with a FINRA member, retention of jurisdiction ceases two years after they are no longer associated with the member. During this two-year period, the registered or associated person is still subject to the rules, regulations, and sanctions (as a result of a customer complaint) FINRA may have imposed during the time which they were registered.

PRE-DISPUTE ARBITRATION CLAUSE UNDER FINRA RULE 2263

Form U4 contains a pre-dispute arbitration clause in item five of Section 15A. It states that most or all disputes must be resolved in arbitration if no agreement is reached in the less binding mediation. When registered representatives sign their Form U4, under item five of Section 15A, they relinquish the right to sue another legal person unless the arbitration declares that they may. Item five further states that alleged discrimination is not covered under the arbitration rules of FINRA, and legal resolution may be sought in another manner. Similarly to discrimination, whistleblowers that have a dispute with their employer are not required to settle the matter under arbitration. Further, the arbitrator's decision is final, with limited opportunity to appeal, and arbitrators are not required to explain the reasoning behind their decisions. In addition to registered individuals being subject to pre-dispute clauses, many FINRA members now require their customers to sign pre-dispute clauses as part of the application process. This allows all customer disputes to be settled in arbitration.

SIPC

The Securities Investor Protection Act established the Securities Investor Protection Corporation, or SIPC. The SIPC is a nonprofit corporation by which paying members' customers are protected against the default of the member firm. All firms that are registered with the SEC and offer a wide range of securities must be SIPC members. The SIPC protects investing customers from the danger of default by their broker/dealer, but it does not guarantee against loss of capital through market movement. Many compare the SIPC to the FDIC, but it is extremely important that customers understand that their funds are not protected under the FDIC. Investors are covered up to $500,000 each, but no more than $250,000 of that may be cash. It should be noted that the $500,000 limit applies to each legal person, so a properly documented trust would also receive $500,000.

When members of the Securities Investor Protection Company, or the SIPC, desire to advertise their affiliation with the SIPC, they must submit to certain rules. Members of the SIPC must have signage in each of their branches with the SIPC logo emblazoned thereon. There must be no indication that the securities may be covered by the FDIC; this is very important if a securities office is located in or near a bank. SIPC members must also disclose if they have concurrent membership in FINRA and/or the NYSE. The signs that are used to display the FINRA, NYSE, and/or SIPC logos should make it clear that the use of the logo indicates registration only, and not an endorsement from any of the three firms. This includes subtle techniques such as using a larger font size for one of the three firms than is used for the name of the member firm.

Supervise the Opening and Maintenance of Customer Accounts

NEW ACCOUNT OPENING
KNOW YOUR CUSTOMER INFORMATION

The registered principal (RP) must approve all new accounts opened by registered individuals under their supervision. Before the RP approves of the account, he should be sure that the required information is present on the new account application. This information is referred to as the "know your customer" information, and includes the customer's full name, social security number, date of birth, phone number, whether or not he or she is a United States citizen (and the country of citizenship if not US), if the customer is associated with another FINRA member, if the account will have margin features, and whether or not he or she is a controlling member of a publicly traded firm.

RESPONSIBILITIES OF THE BROKER/DEALER UNDER THE USA PATRIOT ACT

The PATRIOT Act was established for all forms of business following the terrorist attacks of September 11, 2001. The PATRIOT act was established to help businesses, especially financial institutions, prevent funneling of funds to terrorist organizations. The PATRIOT Act requires that financial institutions establish and maintain a customer information program (or CIP). The minimum required information for collection for CIPs consists of the customer's name, address, social security number, and date of birth. Per the requirements of the USA PATRIOT Act, it is the responsibility of the FINRA member opening a new account to confirm that the customer is who they say they are (usually via some form of government issued identification), retain the method used to determine the customer's identity, and ensure that the person is not on the Office of Foreign Assets Control (OFAC) list. The OFAC list contains the names of individuals and organizations with ties to terrorism.

ENSURING CUSTOMERS UNDERSTAND INVESTMENT AND POTENTIAL RISKS

Not only is it the duty of the registered individual to ensure that all recommendations to customers are suitable to their goals and needs, the registered person is also responsible to educate the customers about the security or product that they are buying. This should include an understandable statement of risks associated with the investment, such as liquidity risk. So that the customers have a reference and understand the risks associated with the investment, all customers must be provided with the unaltered prospectus of the security that they are purchasing. In this case, altering includes any marks on the prospectus, including highlighting of points of interest. The registered person should provide all material information available about the security. This should include negative news about the security that may inhibit the broker's likelihood of selling the security.

PROPER DISCLOSURE OF FEES FOR RESTRICTED AND UNREGISTERED SECURITIES

The nature of restricted and/or unregistered securities makes them more expensive for the FINRA member to properly process. The legal landscape surrounding restricted securities can require many man hours to navigate. For FINRA members to remain profitable, these expenses are usually passed on to the customer. It is important that the registered principal (RP) train the registered representatives (RR) under their supervision on the importance of full disclosure of these fees. Occasionally, the fees for the service will outweigh the benefit that the customer receives (usually in the case of small transactions), and it is the job of the RR to point this fact out to the customer before the customer initiates the transaction.

CUSTOMER FREE CREDIT BALANCES

A broker or dealer is not to use the funds from any customer's free credit balance in connection with the operation of the broker's or dealer's business, unless there have been established adequate procedures under which a customer is sent, every three months, a written statement informing him of the amount due to the customer on the statement date. The broker or dealer shall also notify the customer that the funds are not segregated and may be used in business operations and that the funds are payable on demand to the customer.

FINRA RULE 2090

Know your customer (FINRA Rule 2090) - members of FINRA are to use reasonable diligence when opening and maintaining accounts for customers, and to get to know essential facts about the customer and concerning the authority of each person acting on behalf of a customer.

FINRA RULE 2111

Suitability (FINRA Rule 2111) - a member must have a reasonable basis to believe that an investment or strategy is suitable for the customer based on the information the member has gained, according to the "know your customer" rule. Pertinent information includes the customer's age, other investments, financial situation, tax status, objectives, experience, investment time horizon, liquidity needs, and risk tolerance. For an institutional customer, the member is to have reasonable belief the customer is capable of evaluating risks and has indicated that it is exercising independent judgment.

FINRA Rule 2111 states that advisers must "have a reasonable basis to believe that a recommended transaction or investment strategy involving a security or securities is suitable for the customer, based on the information obtained through the reasonable diligence of the [firm] or associated person to ascertain the customer's investment profile." Thus, Rule 2111 reinforces the need for the registered person to gather complete and accurate suitability information regarding time horizon, liquidity needs, and risk tolerance. The advisor's diligence should include a mutually exclusive analysis of time horizon and liquidity needs as well. While those with a long time horizon may be well positioned to accept the risks associated with liquidity, their goals and desires may require that they have liquidity to invest in other securities.

The term "suitability" refers to information pertaining to the investor's individual monetary situation and psychology. When a registered person is gathering suitability information, he collects such information as the client's investment experience (important to determine if the client understands some of the risks he may be taking); his tolerance for taking risks; time horizon and liquidity needs; and the outcome that he desires in addition to empirical numbers such as the client's net worth, tax bracket, income, and any dependents that he may have. Without this information, the registered person may not make recommendations, but he may still accept unsolicited orders. It is important to understand the client's suitability information to ensure that the registered person makes appropriate recommendations to the client based on his or her unique situations and goals. Illiquid investments may work against a client with a short time horizon, but in favor of a client with a long time horizon.

FINRA RULE 2130

Approval procedures for day-trading accounts (FINRA Rule 2130) - a day-trading member may not open an account for a non-institutional customer without furnishing to the customer a risk disclosure statement and without having approved the customer's account for day trading according to certain criteria. In lieu of approving the customer's account, the member can obtain a written agreement from the customer stating the customer does not intend the account to use for day-trading activities.

FINRA RULE 2270

Day Trading Risk Disclosure Statement (FINRA Rule 2270) - in addition to providing the customer with the risk disclosure statement, the member must post the same disclosure on the member's website. The risks disclosures include: day trading is extremely risky; be cautious of claims of large profits from day trading; day trading requires knowledge of securities markets; day trading requires knowledge of a firm's operations; day trading will generate substantial commissions, even if the per trade cost is low; day trading on margin or short selling may result in losses beyond your initial investment; and potential registration requirements.

REGISTRATION AND DELIVERY INSTRUCTIONS AVAILABLE TO CLIENTS OPENING NEW ACCOUNTS

The types of registration and delivery instructions from which an investor may choose when he opens an account are "hold in street name," "transfer and hold in safekeeping," "transfer and ship," and "delivery versus payment." The most common option for clients using a broker/dealer is for the securities to be held in street name. Securities that are held in street name are nominally registered to the broker/dealer, but are actually owned by the client. This is the most common type of registration because it is the most efficient and convenient form of transacting securities. The "transfer and ship" designation describes the process of transferring ownership to the client and then delivering the security. "Transfer and hold in safekeeping" refers to a process by which the purchasing client is named the new owner of the securities, but the broker/dealer holds the securities for safekeeping. "Delivery versus payment" describes a method whereby the client requests that his securities be delivered to a bank, which will then pay the broker/dealer for the securities.

REVIEWING CUSTOMER ACCOUNTS
ENSURING INVESTMENTS ARE CONSISTENT WITH OBJECTIVES AND RISK TOLERANCE

When customers enter a contractual basis with a FINRA member, they are entitled to a continual monitoring of their accounts to ensure that their goals are being pursued to the best of the member's ability. While initial investments may have been suitable to certain goals, occurrences outside of the member's control may happen to affect the allocation of the customer's account, which in turn can change the suitability of the investments that the customer holds. A conservative customer's account may be made to be more aggressive due to a bull market, wherein his equity holdings experience large growth, and his fixed income holdings experience

34

contraction. To help the client's account remain suitable to his needs, his advisor (with customer permission) may "rebalance" the account, or make trades to bring it back to the original allocation. The registered principal should regularly monitor accounts to make sure that they remain suitable to the customer's original risk tolerance and goals.

PROPER TRADING AUTHORIZATION, EXCESSIVE TRANSACTIONS, AND SUITABILITY ISSUES ON THE SAME DAY TRADES ARE PLACED

Same-day trade review affords the registered principal (RP) key advantages in monitoring customer accounts for irregularities. If a customer's advisor is trading in the customer's account without proper authorization, same-day review allows the RP to identify the situation and remedy it with potentially less impact than if the advisor were to continue doing so. The same is true of the RP catching excessive transactions, also called churning. Most FINRA members have resources that automatically generate reports of unusual activity in accounts. Because the RP reviews and approves trades on a daily basis, reviewing these reports will help the RP catch churning before it becomes a recurring issue with an advisor. While in the process of reviewing the day's trades, RPs should also check for suitability issues which can arise if an advisor is placing all of his or her customers in the same investments. Again, the RP will have access to automated reports that flag such activity.

MSRB RULE G-19

MSRB Rule G-19 requires that, prior to trading in a retail customer's account, the registered individual must collect suitability information regarding the customer's financial status, tax status, investment objective concerning the municipal security being traded, and any other information that might be required to ensure that the transaction meets the customer's suitability needs. The claim that the security is a suitable investment must be supported by complete and accurate information obtained from the customer for that purpose, and information provided by the issuer. MSRB G-19 also addresses suitability issues concerning discretionary accounts, and requires that the investment be suitable in such accounts. Finally, G-19 expressly forbids churning in accounts through multiple transactions, or unreasonably large transactions to provide larger commissions to the registered person.

CHURNING

Churning describes the practice of placing an abnormally large number of transactions in a client's account for the sole purpose of generating additional commissions for the representative. Churning is never ethical, even if the transactions result in a gain in the client's account, although it usually results in losses because the client is paying more fees and commissions than normal. Accounts in which the registered representative of the account has discretionary trading authority are particularly susceptible to churning because the registered individual does not need to have the client's permission to make transactions. It is one of the duties of the registered principals to ensure this does not happen.

Accounts with discretionary trading agreements should be closely monitored for potential churning activities. Fee-based accounts, in which the client pays no commission, but instead a fee based on the total assets under management, are immune to churning by definition.

UTMA/UGMA Accounts

The task of properly handling UTMA/UGMA accounts falls to the accounts' fiduciaries. Because accounts for minors are by definition opened for inexperienced investors, it is a violation of the fiduciary duty for the custodian to take aggressive risks and/or use complex investments that are difficult to understand. As such, UTMA/UGMA accounts must be cash-only accounts (no margin), gains and dividends must be reinvested, the investment must be suitable to the minor, options may not be purchased (the only options allowed are covered calls), and rights and warrants may not be held. It is important to know that the gifts to UTMA/UGMA accounts may not be rescinded, and must be in the form of cash or un-margined securities. Separate accounts must be established for separate beneficiaries (but one beneficiary can have multiple accounts), and the beneficiary may sue for mismanagement of the account. The parents of the minor beneficiary do not control the account unless they are also the custodian of the account.

Documentation When Opening a Wrap Account

In the process of opening a wrap account for a customer, the FINRA member employee should collect and retain information that is normally collected in the process of setting up a new account. This information should satisfy the requirements of the USA PATRIOT Act with personal information such as the customer's full name, date of birth, Social Security number, and non-P.O. box physical address, among others. In the new account document for a wrap account, the fee that is going to be charged to the customer should be plainly disclosed, as well as the frequency with which it will be charged. The employee who sets up the account should obtain the customer's signature and the date that the document was signed. Prior to the account being opened, the customer should be provided with the advisor's form ADV. Form ADV should be provided each time an advisor establishes an advisory relationship with a client.

Correct Handling of Accounts of Decedents and Persons Declared Mentally Incompetent

The registered principal is responsible for the review of the handling of accounts of persons that are declared incompetent or have deceased. While it is the responsibility of the member employee who services the affected customer's account to take all of the necessary steps, the registered principal should be aware of the necessary steps to be taken so that they may perform effective reviews and correct employees when necessary. In the event of the death or incompetence of a client, the member employee should freeze the accounts of the individual until the estate is settled through the receipt of proper documentation (i.e., wills, death certificate), and the estate's executor (or responsible party in the event of declared incompetence) has filed the necessary documentation. No transactions should take place in the accounts during this time.

DIFFERENCE IN ACCOUNTS REGISTERED AS TENANTS-IN-COMMON AND JOINT TENANTS WITH RIGHTS OF SURVIVORSHIP

Accounts registered as tenants-in-common (TIC) and joint tenants with rights of survivorship (JTWROS) are both types of joint account ownership. They are similar in that generally all parties who share ownership of the account have equal rights to the assets in the account; they share the same percentage of ownership and may transact in the account. Under the JTWROS registration, when an owner of the account passes away, the decedent's share of the assets are equally added to the remaining owners' share. As an example, a JTWROS account with three owners assigns 33.33 percent ownership to each owner. If one of the owners passes away, each remaining owner would now possess 50 percent of the value of the account. An account with TIC ownership, however, would not assign the owner's value to the other owners. In the event of the passing of an owner in a TIC account, his portion of the account would be distributed to his estate.

FIDUCIARY ACCOUNTS

Fiduciary accounts are accounts that are established for an owner, but a third party acts as the responsible party with the same rights and responsibilities of an owner. The most common types of fiduciary accounts are trust accounts and accounts benefiting minors, such as UGMA and UTMA accounts. Opening a fiduciary account is similar to the new account process, but in addition to the owner's information, the member firm must also collect the same information for the fiduciary, and the fiduciary responsibility must be outlined in the new account document. The fiduciary of the account must manage the account reasonably and according to the suitability requirements of the owner of the account. This is known as the prudent investor or prudent man rule. The rule of prudence means that the fiduciary should handle the account as if he or she were the owner of the account, and not take unnecessary risks.

SEC RULE 144

Because the registration process of new securities is usually prohibitively expensive for retail investors, the SEC simplified the process for them via Rule 144. If the issuers of the unregistered security reports quarterly and annually to the SEC, then after the owners of the security have held it for at least six months, they may sell it without volume restriction unless they are an affiliate of the issuer. An issuer affiliate is defined as a person or persons who hold 10 percent or more of outstanding shares in a company, directors, control persons, and officers of the issuer. An affiliate of the issue may sell shares of the company after a six-month holding period, but they are subject to volume restrictions, and must file form 144 with the SEC. The 90-day volume restrictions are either one percent of the issued shares or the average trading volume of the security for the prior four weeks, whichever is greater.

SEC Rule 144A

The SEC created Rule 144A to create liquidity for unregistered securities that were issued under Regulations D and S, thus establishing a secondary market for unregistered securities. The investor must be deemed a qualified institutional buyer in order to participate in a Rule 144A transaction. A qualified institutional buy, or QIB, is defined as one with an investment portfolio greater than or equal to $100 million. Usually the types of customers that fall under this definition are investment companies, insurance companies, pension funds, and other types of very large employer-provided retirement plans. FINRA members may achieve QIB status at $10 million. When investors are considered a QIB, they may transact in unregistered securities regardless of holding period and volume.

Form 144

Form 144 is a form to be filed in conjunction with Securities and Exchange Commission (SEC) Rule 144. It must be filed for the sale of more than 5,000 shares or $50,000 of restricted stock in a 90-day period. Form 144 is triggered for filing when affiliates of an issue of restricted stock wish to sell some of their holdings. An affiliate is defined in relation to the issuer as a control person, officer, director, or a person who owns at least 10 percent of the issued shares. In the event that an affiliate wishes to sell more than 5,000 shares or $50,000 worth of their holdings in the company, then it must file Form 144 and submit to the volume rules pertaining thereto.

Day Trading

Day trading describes the practices of trading securities intraday to take advantage of changes in the price (usually of stocks, heretofore referred) to reap short-term gains. Day trading can lead to high fees for the customer that can quickly eat into returns that the client has secured. Additionally problematic is that short-term capital gains on the stocks that are traded are taxed at a higher rate than long-term capital gains. Advisors should not day trade in a client's account. The higher fees generated by the day trading and intraday drops in stock prices can negatively impact the client's account, and it is the advisor's duty to educate the client about the risks of such strategies. If a client insists on day trading, then the advisor should point him or her towards a non-advised low-trading-fee brokerage account.

Regulations for Cash on Delivery Orders

FINRA Rule 11860 prohibits cash on delivery transactions for securities unless the transaction adheres to a strict set of rules. Before the transaction is entered into, the FINRA member must be aware that the transaction will be cash on delivery, the transaction should be marked as such, and the customer must receive a confirmation of the transaction by the end of the next business day. The FINRA member must receive a signed agreement from the customer stating that the "customer will furnish his agent instructions with respect to the receipt or delivery of the securities involved in the transaction promptly upon receipt by the customer of each confirmation, or the relevant data as to each execution" to help ensure that good and prompt delivery is made.

MARKING TO THE MARKET

If pursuant to a securities contract, a party in a transaction finds itself unsecured due to a change in the market price of an asset, that party can demand the contra-party to make a deposit equal to the difference between the market price and the contract price. If the market price changes again as to allow for a refund of the deposit, such refunds are to be made on demand. If these rules are not followed by a party, the other party is entitled to close the contract by making an offsetting purchase or sale contract.

REGULATION T MAINTENANCE CALLS

Under Regulation T, customers with margin accounts must have equity in their accounts of at least 50 percent of their initial purchase. After they meet the initial 50 percent requirement, the values of the securities may move downward until there is only 25 percent equity in the account before they will be required to meet a maintenance call. The FINRA member will issue a maintenance call if the equity value falls below 25 percent. To meet the maintenance call, the customer may deposit cash and/or fully paid securities (other margined securities are not acceptable) into the account in an amount that will bring the equity of the account back above the 25 percent threshold. Additionally, the margined securities may be sold (at a loss to the customer) to bring the equity percentage back up.

HYPOTHECATION OF CUSTOMERS' SECURITIES FOUND IN RULE 15C2-1
GENERAL PROVISIONS

A broker or dealer is prohibited from hypothecating any securities carried in the account of a customer if the circumstances permit:

- the commingling of the customer's securities with other customer's securities, without the written consent of the customers
- the securities to be commingled with the account of another person that is not a bona fide customer of the broker or dealer
- the securities to be hypothecated for an amount that exceeds the total indebtedness of all customers in respect of securities carried for their accounts

AGGREGATE INDEBTEDNESS

Aggregate indebtedness - is not to be reduced because of uncollected items. To calculate, related guaranteed and guarantor accounts are treated as a single account, and balances carrying both long and short positions are adjusted by treating the market value of the securities required to cover any short position as though the market value were a debit.

DIFFERENCES IN TRADITIONAL, ROTH, AND COVERDELL IRAs

IRAs, or individual retirement accounts, were established to incentivize individuals to save for retirement. IRAs are tax advantaged investing accounts that legally allow investors to manipulate their taxable income. In the case of traditional IRAs, as long as the individual meets income limitations, the investor may deduct allowable contributions to his IRA from his taxable income. When the investor begins taking distributions during retirement, however, all of the distributions are taxable. Roth IRAs differ from traditional IRAs in that the investor may not write off allowable contributions, but all distributions taken during retirement are non-taxable. Coverdell IRAs are known as education IRAs. Coverdell accounts allow individuals to set aside money for education and let it grow, tax deferred. The contributions are made with after-tax dollars, but taxes on gains are deferred until they are withdrawn. If the money is withdrawn for qualified higher-education expenses, it is not taxable at all.

WARRANTS

Warrants are rights issued to investors that give them the right to purchase a security at a set price for a certain period of time. Warrants are similar to call options, but differ in that warrants are issued by the issuer of the underlying security instead of sold by another investor. The customer may exercise the warrants and buy the security at the offered strike price, or they may sell the warrant on an exchange to another customer that wishes to buy it. An adviser should consider an individual's specific suitability when making recommendations regarding warrants. If the client is an unsophisticated investor, it may be in his best interests to immediately exercise the rights or sell them to another investor. If the client is suited to a more sophisticated strategy, it may be in his best interests to hold warrants for speculation on the movement of the underlying security.

NASDAQ OMX PHLX RULE 1026

The NASDAQ OMX PHLX rules establish the allowance of options trading on so-called Alpha Indexes. These Alpha Indexes measure the return of an individual security while benchmarking to another (usually comparable) security. The rules go on to further regulate the trade of these options (such as positions limits), and describe the clearing of these trades. PHLX Rule 1026 was established to ensure that Alpha Index options are only sold to customers who are sophisticated enough and have the investment experience required to understand the risks that they have assumed. PHLX Rule 1026 further discusses suitability by requiring that the customer is "capable of... bearing the risks associated with trading in the instruments." This implies that the customer must be able to meet responsibilities associated with options trading, such as having enough cash to cover a put that he has sold and not be fiscally ruined if he has to pay that cash out.

REVIEW OF MANAGED ACCOUNTS TO ENSURE GOALS ARE BEING PROPERLY SERVICED

When a registered individual engages in a contractual relationship with a customer, the adviser should develop a course of action that best suits the needs and desires of the customer. In order to facilitate this, the adviser should develop an investment policy statement, or IPS, with the customer. The investment policy statement then governs how the account should be managed. It is crucial to review managed accounts periodically because even if the IPS is followed initially, market movement may change the allocation of the account to work counter to the customer's goals. If a client's account is out of balance with the goals and objectives, then the adviser may affect what is known as a rebalance. Rebalancing an account is the act of bringing the allocation back to the originally agreed upon asset allocation.

DUTY TO ENSURE PRODUCT KNOWLEDGE

For advisers to meet their customers' needs, it is crucial that they have a well-developed knowledge of the products that are offered. While advisers must be studious to maintain this knowledge, it is the duty of the registered principal to ensure that the individuals under their supervision are provided with access to training material and to encourage them to use it. The registered principal should develop a plan using the training material and implement the plan so that the registered individuals under their supervision are up to date on specific product types and features, and account types and features. An example of this is the contribution limits to IRAs, which tend to increase annually.

NONQUALIFIED AND QUALIFIED RETIREMENT PLANS

Nonqualified retirement plans differ from traditional qualified plans in many ways. Because it is generally only high net worth or highly compensated individuals that have access to the nonqualified plans, there is less emphasis on the protection (i.e., ERISA) of investors in the nonqualified plan because they are assumed to be more sophisticated investors, and typically all of their retirement assets are not attached exclusively to the plan. Additionally, there are no anti-discrimination policies associated with the plans. Where qualified plans benefit from tax advantages, nonqualified plan participants may not write off contributions, thus the IRS does not need to approve the plan and only gains in the account are taxable at withdrawal. The accumulation of assets in nonqualified plans is not necessarily deferred the way qualified plans are. Finally, nonqualified plans do not set up a trust at creation as qualified plans do. The most common nonqualified retirement plan is the deferred compensation plan.

SUITABILITY ISSUES WHEN RECOMMENDING OPTIONS STRATEGIES

Options strategies can range in risk from the ultra-conservative covered call option writing, to ultra-speculative strategies such as naked or uncovered calls. The foremost suitability consideration when recommending options strategies should be the customer's experience with options investing. If they have never before used options, it may be best to start them with covered calls and explain the benefits and the risks of covered call writing. If the client has more experience with options strategies, then the advisor should have a discussion with the client in which they discuss the client's tolerance for risk, and make sure the client understands the potential outcomes of each investment and why the strategy is being used. Clients should also be positioned to be able to meet any cash requirements that arise of options being exercised, without causing a liquidity crisis for the client.

MONITORING CUSTOMER ACCOUNTS

When a registered individual assumes an advisory role with a retail investor, it is his duty to consider the customer's whole financial situation from current income to long-term goals. This includes a thorough analysis of all of his investments, even those not held with his broker/dealer. This will help ensure that the adviser makes suitable recommendations based on the customer's whole situation. Further, registered principals should monitor for such actions as short-term mutual fund trading, guaranteeing against loss (whether a monetary guarantee or some other inducement), using aliases for themselves or customers to circumvent rules, fraud, transacting in the customer's account without their approval or third party authorization, and making recommendations to customers that might compromise their liquidity beyond a reasonable degree.

PREVENTING THE MISUSE AND ABUSE OF CUSTOMER FUNDS

Given the registered individual's relationship with his clients, he or she is uniquely placed to take advantage of a client's trust. The registered principal (RP) should closely monitor accounts for unusual activity such as sending client funds to unrelated third parties or the deposit of a client's fully paid securities to one of the registered individual's margin accounts. While the registered person may fully intend to return the securities or funds to the client, this is illegal in all cases regardless of intent. Additionally, the RP should closely monitor any account that a registered individual and a customer shares. Potential pitfalls of account sharing include the adviser taking disproportionately large gains or losses in the account. While taking more gains than his or her share is obviously unethical, taking larger losses can be viewed as guaranteeing against loss.

SUPERVISORY PLAN FOR FINRA MEMBERS

For FINRA members to remain in good standing with FINRA, they must create a written supervisory plan of procedures. It is the duty of the registered principals of the firm to ensure that all staff members comply with the supervisory procedures. The principals should create and implement training programs to help FINRA member employees understand the supervisory procedures. For the written plan to meet FINRA's standards, it must establish a system by which registered principals are appointed (after meeting FINRA requirements) to ensure that employees are following the plan, designate OSJ branches as responsible for review of other branches, develop a written procedure for examination of operations at branch offices, and establish a means by which potential red flags are identified. Finally, the plan should accommodate regular risk analysis of the firm.

MONITORING FINRA MEMBER'S EMPLOYEES' ACCOUNTS FOR UNUSUAL ACTIVITY

As the supervisor, it is the duty of the registered principal (RP) to use all tools at his disposal to prevent illegal activities in his employees' accounts. Most FINRA member firms have software to generate reports of irregular activity in an employee's account. It is critical that the RP prevent abuse and illegal activity in employees' accounts; the FINRA member employees are the public face of the company, and illegal activity can damage the firm's reputation as well as the offending employee's reputation. Such illegal activity may include misappropriation of client funds for their own account, market manipulation, trading ahead, trading on non-public inside information, and many other potentially disastrous illegal activities.

42

SUITABILITY OF PURCHASE OF RESTRICTED SECURITIES

Restricted securities have several characteristics that can make them complicated to ensure that they are and remain suitable securities for a client. Restricted securities may carry more risk than an issue that has been registered with the Securities and Exchange Commission (SEC) through an initial public offering (IPO). The rigorous underwriting process through which the SEC puts new issues tends to make the issue more transparent, and there is less risk of default and loss of capital. Restricted securities also tend to be illiquid. Whereas a stock that has gone through an SEC IPO trades daily on exchanges (creating instant liquidity), restricted issues are subject to multiple rules regarding their sale and volume of trading. This may create a liquidity issue when the customer needs to access the funds. Generally, only customers whose suitability calls for aggressive risk with a long time horizon are good candidates for restricted securities.

SUPERVISING TRANSACTIONS IN RESTRICTED SECURITIES ON AN ONGOING BASIS

Restricted transactions present a unique set of challenges for registered principals (RP) supervising registered representatives (RR). Restricted securities can generate a lot of conversation and excitement among customers, especially if a restricted security is rumored to be considered an initial public offering. This can lead to customers pressuring the RR to buy a restricted security for them that may not be suitable. The RP is responsible for ensuring that the RR has the proper training and tools to be able to handle suitability questions concerning restricted issues. If the RR advises the customer against a restricted issue, and the customer insists on purchasing it, the RP should provide the RR with the tools to properly document the RR's objection. Furthermore, the RP should monitor trades in restricted securities to ensure that the RR is not pushing the security (as a favor to another customer that might wish to sell the restricted issue) to those for whom it might not be a suitable recommendation.

TRANSFERENCE OF CUSTOMERS' SECURITIES

Customers who wish to transfer securities from one FINRA member to another may submit an automated customer account transfer form, or ACAT. Per FINRA Rule 11870, each FINRA member must "expedite and coordinate activities" to comply with the customer's request. Rule 11870 also provides for non-ACAT transfers via non-ACAT forms. ACAT forms will vary from member to member, but will generally contain the same information. The member that receives the instructions must validate (declare valid) the request or claim that the request is not valid (take issue) within one business day. After that, they must act in a reasonably speedy manner to facilitate the request. If the ACAT requests that the securities be liquidated first, it will generally take longer to process.

WRITTEN SUPERVISORY PROCEDURES

Each FINRA member must have written supervisory procedures. It is important that registered principals (RPs) assist the registered representatives (RRs) under their supervision in understanding the procedures through training and monitoring their activities for violations. Written procedures not only allow members to remain compliant with FINRA, but also help prevent activities that could potentially damage the member's reputation. FINRA requires that each member's procedures include (but are not necessarily limited to) the following guidelines: RPs must be appointed to monitor and enforce the procedures, branches must be identified as offices of supervisory jurisdiction (or OSJs) with RPs on staff to supervise and audit other branches, an inspection program for administration at each branch must be implemented, risk analyses must be performed, and there must be a system in place to monitor red flags.

MSRB RULE G-8

RECORDS FOR MUNICIPAL SECURITY TRANSACTIONS WHEN THE BROKER/DEALER ACTS AS AN AGENT

Municipal Securities Rulemaking Board Rule G-8 section (a) describes the information that must be retained regarding transactions in which broker/dealers act as agents or principals. In transactions in which the broker/dealers act as agents, they must record the terms and conditions of the transaction, the account in which the transaction occurred, time and date the order was placed, the name of the dealer from whom the securities were purchased, price at which the transaction was executed, time and date the order was executed, and the name and address of the person entering the order if the order was entered on someone else's behalf. In the event of a cancellation of an agency transaction, the broker/dealer should retain the terms and conditions and time and date of the cancellation request.

RECORDS FOR MUNICIPAL SECURITY TRANSACTIONS WHEN THE BROKER DEALER ACTS AS A PRINCIPAL

When broker/dealers effect municipal securities transactions as principal, Municipal Securities Rulemaking Board Rule G-8 requires them to record and maintain certain data associated with the transaction. They should record (usually via a trade ticket) the price of the security at the time the transaction was executed, and the date and time of the execution of the order. When broker/dealers act in a principal capacity and effect transactions with a customer, they must maintain a record of the terms and conditions of the transaction, time and date of the order entry, the account in which the transaction was effected, and the name and address of the person entering the order if the order was entered on someone else's behalf.

REQUIRED MAINTENANCE OF CONFIRMATION AND CERTAIN OTHER NOTICES TO CUSTOMERS

Municipal Securities Rulemaking Board (MSRB) Rule G-8 describes the MSRB's rules for keeping records with the preface "every broker, dealer and municipal securities dealer shall make and keep current the following books and records, to the extent applicable to the business of such broker, dealer or municipal securities dealer." Regarding confirmations and certain other notices to customers, Rule G-8 requires that broker/dealers maintain a copy of "all confirmations of purchase or sale of municipal securities, sales or redemptions of municipal fund securities," written disclosures given to customers, and "all other notices sent to customers concerning debits and credits for municipal securities" and all other balances associated with municipal securities transactions.

MSRB Rule G-15

INFORMATION GIVEN TO CUSTOMERS FOR CONFIRMATIONS OF TRANSACTION

MSRB Rule G-15 provides specific guidelines for the information that must be provided on customer confirmations. That information includes the names of all parties involved and any compensation that they may have received, name and address of the broker/dealer and customer, whether it was a purchase or sale, the principal or agency status of the broker/dealer, time and date of the execution of the order, par value of the securities transacted (total price in the case of municipal fund securities), settlement date, yield, dollar price of the security when the transaction was executed, the name of the issuer, the CUSIP number, maturity date and interest rate, dated date, description of the securities transacted, and any required disclosures.

FORMAT OF CONFIRMATIONS

In order to provide standard and easily readable confirmations to customers, the MSRB included guidelines in MSRB Rule G-15 (E) on which broker/dealers should base their confirmation layouts. The required information listed previously to part (E) should appear clearly and in plain language on the front of the confirmation. Exceptions to this rule may be placed on the back of the confirmation and include the required disclosures, the information regarding the customer to whom the securities were sold or from whom they were purchased, and information regarding the time of execution. The other information required to be on confirmations is deemed more important for the customer to easily be able to locate, and thus required to be placed on the front of the confirmation.

REQUIREMENTS OF DVP/RVP

MSRB Rule G-15 prohibits delivery versus payment/receipt versus payment (DVP/RVP) transactions unless they comply with the instructions outlined therein. Rule G-15 states that the broker/dealer must collect the name and address of the agent and the customer's account number with the agent prior to order entry. Also, the order ticket should document the fact that the transaction will be executed as DVP/RVP, the broker/dealer must provide the customer with a confirmation of the transaction at or prior to execution, the customer must provide the broker/dealer with delivery instructions that may be reasonably executed by settlement date, and the customer must also provide his or her agent with instructions that are acceptable to the clearing firm that will accept delivery.

REQUIRED BOOKS AND RECORDS

According to SEC Rule 17a-3 regarding records to be made by certain exchange members, the following are books and/or records that brokers and dealers are required to maintain:

- Memorandum of each brokerage order given or received for the purchase or sale of securities (for customer and firm accounts) - whether executed or unexecuted. The memorandum is to show the terms and conditions; the account for which entered; the time the order was received; the time of entry; the price it was executed; the identity of any associated persons responsible for the account; the identity of the person who entered or accepted the order; and the time of execution or cancellation.
- Memorandum of each purchase and sale for the account of the firm - including the price, the time of execution, and if the transaction was with a customer other than a broker or dealer, a memorandum of each order received showing the time of receipt, the terms and conditions; the identity of each associated person responsible for the account; and the identity of the person who entered or accepted the order.
- Blotters or other records of original entry - are to contain an itemized daily record of all purchases and sales of securities, all receipts and deliveries of securities, all receipts and disbursements of cash, as well as all other debits and credits.
- Copies of customer confirmations - and copies of notices of all other debits and credits for accounts of customers.
- Identification data on beneficial owners of all accounts - all cash and margin accounts are to have identification data including the name and address of the beneficial owner of the account.
- Ledgers or other records reflecting all assets and liabilities - including income and expense and capital accounts.

RECORDKEEPING FOR CORRESPONDENCE WITH AND COMPLAINTS FROM CUSTOMERS

FINRA defines correspondence as any written communication with customers and/or consumers that is not achieved through mass media. While prior approval is not required for correspondence or group correspondence, FINRA member firms are required to keep records of correspondence with customers. Written correspondence and group correspondence (including electronic correspondence) must be retained for three years. Likewise, a customer complaint, which FINRA defines as written communication from a customer alleging misuse or abuse regarding a securities transaction, must be kept on file at the corresponding office of supervisory jurisdiction, or OSJ. Records of customer complaints must be filed with FINRA by the end of the quarter in which it was submitted, and must be retained by the FINRA member for at least four years.

GOOD DELIVERY REQUIREMENTS OF MUNICIPAL SECURITIES

For the delivery of physical municipal securities (i.e., certificate form) to meet good delivery requirements, they must be in good form. Good form includes the certificate, a delivery ticker, and correct denominations of the security. Good form denominations of bearer bonds include $1,000 or $5,000 denominations, while registered bonds may be delivered in any denomination of $1,000 up to $100,000. Additionally, insured bonds must come with proof of insurance. Municipal bonds that have legal opinions written about them must come with those legal opinions. In the event that the seller delivers the securities before the settlement date, the buyer is allowed to reject the securities. In the same vein, if the seller delivers on the settlement date, the buyer is required to accept the delivery.

RESPONDING TO CUSTOMER CLAIMS ABOUT LACK OF RECEIPT OF INTEREST PAYMENTS ON MUNICIPAL BONDS

In the event that an issuer or his paying agent mistakenly pays the interest due on a municipal bond to a former owner of one of their securities, the customer that was entitled to receive the interest payment may inform his broker/dealer of the lack of payment. The buying broker/dealer should then file an interest payment claim with the issue on his customer's behalf. The dealer that sold the securities must pay the customer the interest due within 10 business days of the receipt of the customer's request. If the customer makes the request more than 60 days after the interest was due, the broker/dealer has 20 business days before he has to pay the buyer.

DELIVERY OF CALLABLE MUNICIPAL SECURITIES

Certain consideration must be given to the delivery of bonds that have been called. If an issuer calls only randomly selected bonds and not the entire issue, it is said to have executed a partial call. A call of the entire issue is called an in-whole call. In the case of an issue that has been partially called, the bonds delivered must not be one of the called bonds for the delivery to be considered a good delivery. In the case of in-whole calls, the seller must notify the buyer that the issue has been called or the delivery is not considered good. An exception to this is if the bonds are called after the trade has been executed, in which case the point is moot because the seller must deliver the bonds regardless of call status.

REGULATION S-P

Regulation S-P (Privacy of Consumer Financial Information) contains at its core three main purposes or functions:

1. The regulation requires financial institutions to notify its customers of its privacy practices
2. The regulation prohibits financial institutions from disclosing nonpublic personal customer information to third parties, unless the institution has disclosed its practices to the customer and the customer has failed to opt out of such disclosure
3. The regulation provides certain industry standards for financial institutions regarding privacy practices and disclosure of customer information

Through the various components of Regulation S-P, customers of financial institutions are afforded additional protection from the distribution of their personal information, while financial institutions are provided with a "road map" to follow to ensure they are staying in compliance with the regulation.

Supervise Sales Practices and General Trading Activities

FINRA MEMBER FIRM'S RESPONSIBILITIES REGARDING CUSTOMER COMPLAINTS

When a customer of a FINRA member firm submits a complaint with the firm regarding a securities transaction, the firm must immediately investigate the matter. Any less grievous matter that is settled between the customer and the member need not be forwarded to FINRA. However, if resolution is not reached, the matter should be forwarded to FINRA's Director of Arbitration and, regardless of customer satisfaction, any complaint of theft or forgery must immediately be forwarded to FINRA. As part of the investigation FINRA may require the associated person to make available information relevant to the claim, provide testimony under oath, and give the investigators copies of related books, records, and accounts. The FINRA member must submit any requested information or records within 20 days of the request, or face possible suspension or revocation of registration.

COMPLAINTS AND RECORDKEEPING REQUIREMENTS

NASD Rule 3110 defines a complaint as a written statement "of a customer or any person acting on behalf of a customer alleging a grievance involving the activities of those persons under the control of the member in connection with the solicitation or execution of any transaction or the disposition of securities or funds of that customer." Rule 3110 also provides direction for keeping records regarding complaints. In their office of supervisory jurisdiction, or OSJ, the member must retain a separate file for all written complaints that customers submit, and the member must document the action that the member took within the file. Also within the file, the member must provide plain instructions on accessing other files (i.e., correspondence) related to the complaint.

TIME FRAMES TO SUBMIT COMPLAINTS TO FINRA MEMBER'S HOME OFFICE

Dependent upon the degree of the complaint submitted, there are multiple time frames to submit the complaint to the firm's main office, and registered persons should know all of them. FINRA members must file written complaints with FINRA by the end of the calendar quarter in which it was received (there is a 15-day grace period). However, if theft or forgery is alleged, they must submit it within 10 days of receipt. Alternatively, those firms with the NYSE as their self-regulatory organization must file all complaints (both oral and written) quarterly. NYSE members must also acknowledge receipt of complaints within 15 business days. For FINRA member firms, complaints regarding options should be immediately submitted to the home office.

FINRA RULE 11890

In the event that a trade is erroneously placed, a trading party may appeal to FINRA to nullify the trade placed. Under Rule 11890, an executive vice president (EVP) of FINRA may review a trade, with or without request from a trader involved, to determine if it is clearly erroneous. The FINRA EVP may nullify the transaction if it is "clearly erroneous," or if it is necessary to maintain a "fair and orderly market or the protection of investors and the public interest." Rule 11890 further defines what is considered a clearly erroneous trade. In the event that FINRA declares a transaction null and void, the "aggrieved party" may file an appeal under Rule 11894.

DUTY OF REGISTERED PRINCIPALS TO REVIEW AND APPROVE TRADES DAILY

One of the most important duties of the registered principal (RP) is the review of trades placed by registered representatives (RR) under their supervision. Review of trades has been greatly simplified by the advent of computer technology, with automated reports generated for the RP to review trades placed by RRs to help the RR catch any obvious error. In addition to assisting the RR in catching errors, the RP is also under obligation to review trades for FINRA violations. During the review process, the RP should also look for violations such as front-running, trading ahead, trading along, interpositioning, churning, and any other potential violation of FINRA regulations. The review of trades by the RP not only protects the retail customer from unethical practices, but also protects the reputation of the FINRA member by detecting and preventing unscrupulous efforts that may be detrimental to the firm's reputation should they continue.

MARKING THE CLOSE

Marking the close, also referred to as portfolio pumping, refers to manipulating the underlying securities of a fund prior to the end of the quarter to make the performance of the fund appear better than it actually is. Managers of mutual funds and exchange-traded funds are well placed to commit such manipulation, as they may manipulate volume and prices with the resources of the funds. Most often, this manipulation cannot be sustained, and the performance of the portfolio balances out, but after the end of the quarter when the performance has already been measured. When performance evens the fund value out, this manipulation can hurt investors who bought the fund at an artificially high price with the (false) knowledge of the quarterly report.

SPECIAL MEMORANDUM ACCOUNTS

Special memorandum accounts, or SMAs (sometimes referred to as excess equity because the 50 percent minimum equity requirement under Regulation T has been exceeded), are created when the value of a security purchased on margin exceeds the amount originally paid for the security. The value of an SMA account is calculated by dividing the excess returns of the margined securities in an account by half. For example, if a $100 investment returned two dollars, the SMA of the account would equal one dollar. When a customer has SMA in his or her margin account, they may either withdraw 100 percent of the SMA account as cash or use 200 percent of the SMA account to purchase other marginable securities.

FRONT-RUNNING

Front-running is the practice of a registered individual benefitting from the knowledge of a customer or multiple customers' placing a block order that may affect the price of the security in question by placing trades on the underlying security in their own accounts. This is unethical in every situation, and bears more than a passing resemblance to insider trading. Front-running is closely regulated by FINRA Rule 5270, and should be monitored closely by all registered principals who are responsible for approving trades. Front-running should be easily identifiable to diligent principals (via automatically generated reports that search for such activity), and appropriate disciplinary action should be taken concerning the individual that committed front-running.

FINRA RULE 11810

If a securities contract is not being completed by the seller, the buyer can close the contract after the third business day, except for in certain instances when the contract is subject to buy-in requirements of the securities exchange, when the contract is exempt by other provisions of the Exchange Act, and when the securities are issued by an investment company or direct participation program. In each instance that a buyer is to use this Rule, a notice of buy-in meeting specific requirements is to be delivered to the seller. This notice is to contain information including date the contract will be closed out, the quantity and value of the securities, the settlement date of the contract, and other material information.

BUY-IN RULES

Regular way settlement for most securities (excluding United Statement Government Securities) is two days. This is often expressed as T+2. When an investor sells a stock, he or she has two days from the date of sale to deliver the securities. If the investor does not deliver the stocks within two days, he is subject to buy-in rules. In a buy-in, the investor's broker/dealer must purchase the securities to deliver them to the buyer. The broker/dealer will pay the market price for the securities, make delivery, and then charge their non-delivering customer whatever price they paid for it. The easiest way for customers to avoid buy-ins is for them to have their securities held in street name, so that their broker/dealer may transact on their behalf and make delivery for them.

FAIR PRICE FOR MUNICIPAL SECURITIES

The Municipal Securities Rulemaking Board (MSRB) established a set of criteria to determine fair market value of securities when being traded in a principal capacity or agency capacity. Because a broker/dealer is considered to be a sophisticated investor and therefore not to need as much protection as a retail investor, when determining the fair value of municipal securities, the broker/dealer should use his best rational processes while considering the time and expense of acquiring the security, remember that he is making the purchase or sale with profit in mind, and give consideration to the total dollar amount of the transaction. When acting on behalf of others, the broker/dealer should consider the time and effort spent to obtain the security, the amount of money spent effecting the transaction, the overall

50

services that he provided, and other expenses (such as commission to the registered individual facilitating the trade) that the transaction generates.

HANDLING NON-PUBLIC INFORMATION REGARDING MUNICIPAL SECURITIES

In much the same manner as dealing in any other security, the Municipal Securities Rulemaking Board, or MSRB, forbids the persons with material non-public information from acting upon that information to effect a securities transaction. Regarding municipal securities, however, a different (often wider range) number and type of people may be privy to non-public material information. Because municipal securities are issued by state and local governments, it is not only officers and directors (and their families) that may have access to inside material information. Many politicians spend long hours considering whether or not a municipal issue may be right for their constituency, and their aides become privy to non-public information from which they could benefit. Those aides quickly become insiders and, as in all other transactions, trading on non-public material information is prohibited.

ORDER OF PRIORITY WHEN FILLING ORDERS FOR NEW MUNICIPAL SECURITY ISSUES

The Municipal Securities Rulemaking Board requires that each underwriting syndicate must set in advance the priority they will give to those wishing to purchase a new issue of municipal securities. While this is not the same in each situation, it must be established during the underwriting and not left to the whim of the underwriters. The most common order of allocation is as follows, from highest priority to lowest priority: presale orders, group net orders, designated orders, and member orders. Presale orders are orders placed before the underwriting syndicate bought the new issue, and are credited to all members of the syndicate. Group net orders are regular customer orders, and are also credited to all members of the syndicate. Designated orders are customer orders that are filled by more than one member, and the customer designates which member fills the order. Member orders are orders that are filled by only a single syndicate member. This structure is usually most successful in assisting all members in filling their selling obligations.

REQUIREMENTS FOR GROUP NET ORDERS OF NEW MUNICIPAL ISSUES

When a broker/dealer places a group net order for a new municipal issue for a customer, he must reveal the identity of the customer, the total value of the securities purchased at maturity, and the maturity date of the securities purchased.

STATEMENTS SENT FOR PERIODIC PURCHASES OF MUNICIPAL FUND SECURITIES

Customers of broker/dealers occasionally instruct them to purchase securities for them on a periodic, recurring basis for the same or similar dollar amount each time. This is referred to as dollar cost averaging, and accomplished (for municipal fund securities) through a period municipal fund security plan. Non-periodic plans give the customer great discretion in the frequency and dollar amount of the purchase. Customers on periodic plans should receive quarterly statements, while non-periodic plan customers should receive monthly statements. Because customers that invest via periodic plans know that the transactions occur regularly in their account, they may instruct the broker/dealer in writing to send them periodic statements instead of confirmations each time a transaction is completed.

REQUIRED DISCLOSURES RELATED TO THE SALE OF MUNICIPAL FUND SECURITIES

When municipal fund security issuers choose to advertise a product, they must provide certain disclosure in each advertisement. Each ad must instruct the audience to read the issuer's official statement for additional relevant information and from where that statement may be obtained. If past performance data are shown, the ad must contain a phone number or website by which the customer may collect current performance data. In the case of 529 plans, the ad must instruct the audience to determine if their state's 529 plan has tax benefits that are not accessible via out of state plans. These are the minimum requirements for all municipal fund securities; while some issuers choose to make more disclosures, none may opt to disclose less information.

MSRB RULE G-13

The Municipal Securities Rulemaking Board established Rule G-13 to require broker/dealers providing quotes on municipal securities to ensure that the quotes are bona fide with the acknowledgement that security prices are subject to change. For the quotation to be bona fide, the dealer must be willing to purchase the security at the price quoted. A bona fide and fair quote takes into account the dealer's inventory of the offering, reasonable acknowledgment of price change, and the firm's other positions in inventory as well. If not otherwise noted, bona fide offers represent firm offers.

MSRB RULE G-31

Municipal Securities Rulemaking Board (MSRB) Rule G-31 was established to prevent municipal securities broker/dealers from using their sales numbers to bring pressure on investment to send them business as compensation for outstanding sales numbers. Conversely, it would result in broker/dealers not dealing with the investment company if they (the investment company) did not send business to the broker/dealers. Both of the preceding situations are counter to the best interests of the customers, which should be the objective of both parties. MSRB Rule G-31 is also referred to as the anti-reciprocal rule, and it was created to prevent broker/dealers from bringing undue pressure to bear on investment companies, and to protect the best interests of the broker/dealers' customers.

DISCRETIONARY ACCOUNTS

In regards to discretionary accounts, excessive transactions, authorization and acceptance of account, approval and review of transactions, and exceptions to the Rule according to NASD Rule 2510 are explained below:

- Excessive transactions - when a member has discretionary powers over the account of a customer, the member may not transact purchases or sales that are in excessive size or frequency in comparison to the size and character of the account.

- Authorization and acceptance of account - a member may not exercise its own discretion in a customer's account unless they have received written authorization from the customer.
- Approval and review of transactions - a member shall quickly and in writing approve all discretionary transactions and regularly review all discretionary accounts to prevent any excessive transactions.
- Exceptions - the Rule does not apply to the time and price that an order received from the customer is executed at, though such orders are only valid through the end of the business day. It also does not apply to certain bulk exchanges of net asset value of money market mutual funds.

SELLING AWAY

The term "selling away" describes the act of a registered individual selling a security that is not offered or approved by the brokerage for which they work. Often, an individual engages in selling away via private placement or real-estate deals. Selling away is a violation of FINRA rules. It is particularly dangerous to FINRA firms because the registered principal does not have oversight of the transaction and cannot guarantee that the transaction is compliant with FINRA rules and regulations. Additionally, there are usually very valid reasons why the FINRA member has chosen not to approve the offering, such as risk to the customer. There are very few cases (if any) in which a FINRA member will make an exception for selling away, and the exception must be given in writing. In the event that a registered representative (RR) feels that the transaction is in the best interest of the customer, the RR should consult with his supervising RP and provide the customer with contact information for a FINRA member that offers the investment. The most common transactions in which selling away occur are private placements. It is the duty of the registered principal (RP) to monitor employee activity to prevent or catch selling away. This may be more difficult than other duties the RP may have because selling away will not automatically generate a report because it did not occur at the employing FINRA member.

RESTRICTIONS PLACED ON COMPENSATION PAID TO RESEARCH ANALYSTS

Rule 2711 places the following restrictions on research analyst compensation:

- Research analysts cannot receive any bonus, salary or other compensation based on a specific investment banking service.
- A committee must review and approve the compensation paid to a research analyst. This review must be performed annually and reported to the member's board of directors.
- Investment banking may not be represented on the compensation review committee.
- The committee must consider the research analyst's performance, the correlation between recommendations and investment performance and recommendations from the member's clients and employees.
- The compensation review cannot take into account the research analyst's contribution to the investment banking business.

53

- The basis for the research analyst's compensation must be documented.
- The committee must make an annual attestation of the review.

ASSISTING CUSTOMERS IN ASSESSING GOALS AND DEVELOPING AN INVESTMENT POLICY STATEMENT

The investment policy statement, or IPS, is a document that establishes how the customer's money should be handled. In order to develop an IPS that is personal and relevant to a customer, several aspects of the customer's experience, tolerances, and goals should be discussed. The adviser should be aware of the investor's time horizon (either the number of years until the client wishes to retire or his overall life expectancy) and tailor the strategy toward that goal. A client with a short time horizon should not be invested in long-term illiquid assets. Further, his IPS should be based upon the customer's investing experience and risk tolerance. An unsophisticated investor with minimal investing experience should not be sold complex products. The adviser should also consider the client's goal concerning the funds that they are investing. Is this account a retirement savings account, or is it purely for speculation? Such questions will lead to widely varying IPSs.

CONCENTRATED POSITION

Registered principals (RPs) should review accounts under their supervision to help prevent customer loss because of concentrated positions. A concentrated position in an investment account is an investment in a security that is disproportionately large compared to the other investments in the account. This may occur for a number of reasons, but the RP should work closely with advisors to ensure this issue is resolved, especially because many advisors tend to work with large numbers of clients, and the RP may be able to identify problematic accounts with a simple report that he or she pulls. Unless the client is insistent upon retaining the concentrated position (i.e., the position is a favorite stock), then concentrated positions can be easily fixed by distributing excess position to the rest of the securities in the account to bring the account back to the original allocation. This is known as rebalancing an account.

TRADING AHEAD OF RESEARCH REPORTS

Trading ahead of research reports occurs when a person expects a security to be affected by the release of a research report. The reasons for the trade determine the ethicality of the trade. If a trade desk is placing the trade based on public knowledge and they only expect a change, then the trades placed are legal and ethical under FINRA Rule 5280. However, if the trade desk is privy to material non-public information concerning the security, whether or not they have non-public access to the research report, a trade would be illegal and unethical according to FINRA Rule 5280. A firm that trades ahead of a research report should document their reasons well, and have proof that the reasons are public knowledge.

MARKET MANIPULATION

Market manipulation is an attempt by a person to artificially maneuver a particular market, whether stock, bond, or currency, for personal gain (or the gain of others) through the use of unethical methods. This is often accomplished by manipulating price and trading volume to make a particular security appear more or less valuable than it really is. Common methods include "painting the tape," in which a group of collaborating violators buy from and sell to each other to create artificial volume, and "pump and dump," in which a large position holder in a company gives false or misleading information about the company to entice other investors to buy in to the company, at which point the larger holder sells out of, or dumps, his position.

INSIDER TRADING

Insider trading is the act of a party buying or selling a position in a company when they are privy to material non-public information. Regulators consider this to be an unfair advantage over the investing public, as the insider may benefit from something that damages retail investors. As an example, the controller of a manufacturing firm that just received a government contract may not buy additional stock in his or her employer's company until it is public knowledge. Insider trading is not always committed intentionally, as the violators may not know that they are considered insiders. Anyone with inside information, whether a director, a director's spouse, or a janitor employed elsewhere, is considered to be an insider, and may not trade on non-public information.

MONITORING ACCOUNTS FOR MARKET MANIPULATION AND INSIDER TRADING

While the average registered individual does not have the means or the resources to commit some of the more egregious forms of market manipulation, they do have the potential to lead customers into insider trading or some form of market manipulation. It is also important that the registered individual help the customer understand restrictions they may have on a large position of stock that may not be traded due to anti-manipulation FINRA regulations. It may also occur that the customer dupes the registered individual into assisting them with insider trading and/or market manipulation. It is the duty of the registered principal to monitor accounts for this type of activity. This may include carefully monitoring trades that the principal is responsible for approving, and having special knowledge of accounts that contain positions that may lead to manipulation or insider trading.

MONITORING ENTRY AND ALLOCATION OF BLOCK ORDERS

There are several potential issues that may arise from the placement of block orders. Block order entries are a convenient way for registered individuals with foreknowledge of the order placement to turn a quick (and unethical) profit by buying or selling the affected security before the block order is placed. This is referred to as trading ahead. Registered principals (RPs) should monitor trading in employees' accounts concerning a specific security that is about to be block traded. Registered principals should also be sure that one of their employees does not unfairly allocate a portion of the buy or sell to one of their customers. Block trades should be filled fairly and by random selection.

TRADING AGAINST FIRM RECOMMENDATIONS AND NON-PUBLIC MATERIAL INFORMATION

New York Stock Exchange Rule 401 calls into question the motive of any member or member affiliate that places a trade in a security that coincides with a recommendation by the firm, either right before or right after the recommendation is made. To avoid the appearance of insider trading, any member or affiliate with non-public knowledge of the security, whether or not it pertains to the firm's recommendation, should abstain from transacting on the security or passing the information along. The member and its affiliates should only transact in the security after the knowledge has been made public, and the information has moved the markets accordingly. This includes all types of transaction on the security, even those that do not follow the advice of the firm's recommendation.

REGULATION SHO

Regulation SHO established a "locate" requirement for securities that are being sold short. According to Regulation SHO, FINRA members must ensure that they have access to the security being sold short (this is often accomplished by checking their own stock of securities for that specific security) so that the customer can readily purchase the security to close the short position. Regulation SHO specifically applies to short sales in equities. In the event that the firm does not have the security in its stock, it may use the securities of customers to satisfy the locate requirement. For purposes of Regulation SHO, their customers are considered to have the security if they currently hold it, own a security that may be converted to the security in question, or if they have exercised rights, warrants, or options on the security.

SELLING SECURITIES SHORT

The term "selling short" refers to the act of a customer selling securities that he or she does not own in hopes that the value of the security will decrease and they may buy the security back at a lower price. This may only be accomplished by the investor borrowing securities from their broker/dealer. The broker/dealer may loan the securities to the investor from their own inventory or from other customers that have margin accounts. Less common methods of locating securities for short sales include borrowing the securities from another FINRA member or institutional investors. Short sales must be affected in margin accounts to assist the FINRA member and the investor in meeting the necessary requirements for short selling. Because short sellers do not own the stock that they are selling, they do not benefit from stock splits or dividends; the lenders receive these benefits.

FINRA RULE 3240

FINRA rules regarding borrowing from or lending to customers (FINRA Rule 3240) are discussed below:

- Permissible lending arrangements; conditions - a person associated with a member is not to borrow money from or lend money to a customer unless the member has written procedures allowing it or the arrangement meets one of the following conditions:

- the customer is part of the person's immediate family
- the customer is a certain type of financial institution
- the customer and the person are both registered persons of the same member
- the arrangement is based on a personal relationship with the customer
- the arrangement is based on a business relationship outside of the broker-customer relationship

- Notification and approval - the member is to be notified of such arrangements and must give written approval, unless otherwise stated in the member's policies.
- Definition of immediate family - includes parents, grandparents, mother and father-in-law, husband or wife, brother or sister, brother or sister-in-law, son or daughter-in-law, children, grandchildren, cousin, aunt or uncle, niece or nephew, and any other person that the person supports.
- Record Retention (Supplementary Material - .01) - the written approval is to be kept for at least three years.

VARIABLE ANNUITIES

Variable annuities are insurance products that guarantee a stream of income in the future. Unlike fixed annuities, variable annuities offer the opportunity of fluctuating streams of income (sometimes higher, sometimes lower) rather than the fixed figure that fixed annuities offer. The stream of income is based upon the underlying investments that the investor chooses for the annuity. Variable annuities may be very attractive to some investors who wish to benefit from market volatility and still have a guaranteed income, but they can be very illiquid with high exit fees if an investor needs liquidity. Additionally, variable annuities pay high up-front commissions to the selling adviser. It is paramount that the customer's suitability is the foremost concern when selling a variable annuity, and not necessarily in the adviser's best interest. Purchasing a variable annuity should not create a liquidity crisis for the client, and the goal should be to receive income from the investment.

1035 EXCHANGES

Section 1035 of the internal revenue code allows for the tax free exchange of insurance products from one company to another. If a registered person feels that the customer may be better served by 1035 exchanging an existing variable annuity to another company, they may recommend that the customer do so. This may be a valid recommendation for many reasons (such as better guarantees at the new firm), but the advisor must also consider all aspects of the exchange so that the customer is not damaged in the process. Many annuities have high surrender charges and can lose a large portion of their initial premium if the money is moved before the surrender period expires. The advisor should consider the client's age and investment experience and new or increased fees that might be incurred. The advisor should also make certain that the product is in the customer's best interest and not his or her own interests, as variable annuities tend to pay very high commissions.

MUTUAL FUND SWITCHING

Mutual fund switching describes the process of moving an investment from one mutual fund to another either inside or outside the same company. Many investment companies offer trading fee discounts and load waivers if the fund is switched within the funds that the investment company offers. The only suitability issue that arises from these types of switches is ensuring that the new fund is right for the customer's objectives. However, if a front-loaded mutual fund is switched multiple times between multiple companies, it may be a sign of a form of churning on the representative's part. Potential risks arise from switching back-loaded products as well, although churning is not one of them. Many investments that are back-loaded come with a CDSC surrender-period in which the customer will be charged a fee to exit the investment. The CDSC period should also be of note when considering a customer's liquidity needs.

ETF

Exchange-traded funds (ETFs) are investment company products that offer an investment strategy that has been bundled into single shares. ETFs undergo an initial public offering and trade on exchanges like individual stocks. The underlying securities of an ETF may be anything from an index (such as the S&P 500) to complex short-selling strategies. Customers should be aware of the potential pitfalls and risks (i.e., higher fees for a strategy that has a large trading volume) associated with each individual ETF that is recommended. An index ETF has little complexity, and the customer is only exposed to regular market risk. However, a complex short-selling strategy may come with much higher fees, and the potential for loss may be much greater. Customers should be made aware of all aspects of the ETF, and the ETF should be suitable to the customer's needs.

OPEN-ENDED MUTUAL FUNDS

Mutual funds are investment company products that are representative of an investment strategy that has been bundled into shares. Mutual funds are in a constant state of issuing new shares and redeeming old ones, similar to a constant initial public offering of securities. The underlying securities of mutual funds range from stocks and commodities to bonds and much more complex strategies. Unlike other similar investment company products, investors may purchase and redeem fractional shares. Because the performance of underlying assets of mutual funds varies widely, mutual funds are priced at the end of the trading day based on the value of the underlying assets. This is referred to as net asset value, or NAV. If an investor wishes to purchase a share of a mutual fund, the investment company responsible for the fund issues a new share for the investor and the investor buys the fund at the day's end NAV. If an investor wishes to sell a mutual fund, the investment company redeems the share (which then ceases to exist) at the day's end NAV.

STATE-ADMINISTERED 529 PLANS AND COVERDELL EDUCATIONAL SAVINGS ACCOUNTS

529 college savings plans and Coverdell Educational Savings Accounts (CESAs) were both established to assist investors who desire to save for a beneficiary's education. While both accounts treat earnings and withdrawals similarly, there are very stark contrasts in their administration. While CESAs have an annual contribution limit of $2,000, 529 plans tend not to have annual contribution limits. CESAs also cut off funding of accounts when the beneficiary reaches age 18, while 529 plans do not have age limits on contributions. Also, CESAs limit the modified adjusted gross income of the contributors, but there is no income limit to contribution to 529 plans. 529s and CESAs are treated similarly when students applied for student tuition aid. 529s also benefit from special gifting rules while CESAs do not.

529 COLLEGE SAVINGS PLANS ESTABLISHED AS MUNICIPAL INVESTMENT FUNDS

One of the types municipal funds that states are allowed to create is the 529 college saving plan. Typically, the issuing state will contract a third party investment company to administer their 529 plans. Individuals may invest money for a beneficiary's education and, if withdrawal stipulations are met, the earnings on the investments are not taxed. Some states offer deductibility status of contributions from state income tax, but usually only if the money is invested in that state's 529 plan. There is a range of investments offered in 529 plans from conservative strategies to aggressive strategies, to age-based strategies that begin aggressively and become more conservative the closer the beneficiary comes to needing the funds. The investor may change investment strategies once per year. The risk associated with 529 plans varies by investment strategy, but the state does not guarantee against loss, so the investor bears the market risk.

DIRECT PARTICIPATION PROGRAMS

Direct participation programs, or DPPs, are investment vehicles by which investors may "participate" directly in the gains and losses of a venture, thereby circumventing the corporate structure associated with more traditional investment vehicles. Investors find DPPs attractive because they may receive tax benefits associated with the cash flow of the DPP that are not available through traditional investments. While investors are a participant in the DPP's capital structure, their participation is passive. DPPs are subject to IRS scrutiny to ensure that the DPP is actually attempting to turn a profit, and not simply to shelter income from taxes. DPPs tend to be very illiquid and can be riskier than publicly traded companies because they do not undergo the scrutiny of an IPO the way a publicly traded company does. Customers whose suitability does not allow for these risks should be steered away from DPPs.

ENSURING SUITABILITY OF INVESTMENTS

Investing is a long-term proposition for most, if not all, retail investors. With that in mind, it is important for the registered individual to review the customer's accounts to ensure that an investment that the customer may have made years ago still suits the customer's needs. It is of immediate importance that the investment is suitable when it is purchased. The registered principal should run reports at his or her disposal to search for specific investments that may have negative suitability implications, and ensure that the investment matches the customer's suitability statements. Further, the principal should monitor accounts on an ongoing basis to ensure that an existing investment does not work counter to the client's updated suitability (for instance, adjusted time horizon and risk tolerance), or that growth or loss in an account has changed the accounts allocation making it unsuitable for the client.

NEW ISSUE OFFERINGS

The term "new issue" describes the process of a firm bringing its stock to market where it will be available to the general public. This is accomplished through a process called the initial public offering, or IPO. For an IPO to be finalized, the issuing firm must submit to a rigorous examination by the Securities and Exchange Commission (SEC). After the IPO is finalized, the SEC will allow the IPO to be sold. To assist with the sale of the securities and the IPO process, issuing firms usually enlist the help of investment banks. Investment banks have sufficient knowledge and resources to navigate the IPO process, and the means by which to bring the securities to market.

RESPONSIBILITIES AND RISKS WHEN DEALING WITH NEW ISSUES

In the event that a registered individual is advising a customer regarding a new issue, that individual should have a conversation with the customer to determine the suitability and legality of purchasing the new issue. The registered individual should ensure first that the customer is not a restricted person and, if the customer is a restricted person, whether or not he may have an exemption to allow him to purchase the new issue. It is also important that the registered person discusses special risks inherent to initial public offerings (IPO), such as the high volatility of what are deemed "hot issues." Hot issue IPOs are IPOs about which there is an excessive amount of "buzz" and can lead to dramatic volatility in a security and result in a large loss of capital.

BLUE SKY LAWS

Given that the nature of blue sky laws is to prevent fraud and protect investors, blue sky laws require that new issues are registered to provide a researchable product and transparency. Issuers of securities that are registered with the Securities and Exchange Commission (SEC) typically conform to state-specific blue sky regulation by filing a notice with the state securities administrator that their securities are registered with the SEC. Additionally, a brokerage and/or their representative must be appropriately registered in their state to offer a new issue. Only when a security is properly registered with the state securities administrator, and the broker brokering the transaction is also duly registered with the state, does the issue and sale of new issues comply with blue sky regulations.

TYPES OF PUBLIC OFFERINGS

In a primary offering, the issuer raises capital to expand operations. The proceeds of the issue go to the issuing firm. In secondary offerings, one or more of the majority stockholders in the firm sell most or all of their holdings in the company to the public. If the company has not already undergone an IPO, secondary offerings may require underwriting. Unlike primary offerings, the proceeds from the sale go to the stockholder, not the issuer. Split offerings, the most common type of public offering, combine the characteristics of secondary and primary offerings. The issuer and the major stock holders both make an offering at the same time, and each receives their prospective proceeds. Shelf offerings refer to the practice of companies holding back a portion of their underwritten securities to be offered at a later date in another public offering.

PROPER FORM FOR ORDER ENTRY TICKETS AND PROPER HANDLING OF CUSTOMER'S ORDER

For an order ticket to be in proper form, it must contain the following information: the customer's account number at the clearing firm, the time and date that the order was accepted, whether it is a buy or a sell and any qualifiers related thereto, whether the sale is long or short, and whether the security has been located for a short sale. A customer's order should be executed as soon as it is received. Any solicited order must be withheld until the adviser has verbal authorization (or written third-party authorization) from the client to proceed. Mutual fund orders are not as time sensitive as stock orders because they are not traded until the end of the day when the net asset value (or NAV) is determined.

DISCLOSURE TO CUSTOMERS REGARDING SECURITIES BEING SOLD

Proper disclosure of the risks and features of a product is vital to ensuring the suitability of an investment. The customer should understand exactly what he is buying, and why it is the correct option given his risk tolerance and objectives. Many investment products have aspects that limit their liquidity, cap their growth, or have a high risk for loss. The FINRA member should educate the customer on these risks and make sure that the customer understands them and how the investments fit into his portfolio. While advertisements or media exposure may catch the customer's attention, such ads often do not disclose all material facts associated with an investment. The selling adviser should explain the material facts of an investment to the customer and provide him with FINRA-member-approved disclosure documents to help ensure the customer understands what he is buying.

DEFERRED COMPENSATION PROFIT SHARING ARRANGEMENTS

A deferred compensation profit sharing arrangement, often shortened to deferred comp, describes a means by which companies may incentivize highly paid employees through profit sharing. Rather than traditional profit sharing, employees receiving deferred compensation receive a promise to be paid a certain amount at a later date. This is attractive to employees because they are still going to receive the amount of money promised, but may benefit from a lower tax bracket when they actually receive the compensation. Employees may wait until retirement and have a reduced income before they take the deferred comp; this has the effect of potentially lowering the tax rate at which the comp is taxed.

MUTUAL FUND BREAKPOINTS

In regards to mutual funds, the term "breakpoint" describes a certain dollar amount at which a mutual fund company will discount the commission charged. Once an investor crosses the breakpoint threshold, he is rewarded with paying lower commissions. It is the duty of the advisor to ensure that the customer knows the threshold and doesn't try to steer him to another investment company so that the advisor may collect a larger commission. Investment companies will even offer the customer discounted commissions if they come close to the breakpoint, but only for as long as the customer signs a letter of intent stating his plans to buy more of the fund (past the breakpoint) at some point in the near future. It is the responsibility of the registered principal to monitor customers to ensure that they are receiving breakpoint discounts and not being steered away to other investment companies to avoid the breakpoint.

EXEMPTION FROM REGISTRATION THAT A REGULATION A OFFERING RECEIVES

Regulation A governs the sale of new issues that are small; "small" in the case of Regulation A is less than $5 million in a 12-month period. Companies often use Regulation A offerings to determine if there is enough demand for their securities to warrant the expense of a long underwriting process to make an initial public offering. Instead of filing the entire registration statement with the Securities and Exchange Commission (SEC), the company will file the abbreviated Form 1-A, called an offering statement. The SEC intends for Regulation A to allow issuers to assess an offering's potential and so will permit the company to issue an offering circular instead of a full prospectus. Any sales material used in conjunction with a Regulation A offering must be filed with the SEC, and the issuer must follow up the issue with Form 2-A, which identifies how much money was raised in the offering and how it will be spent.

REGULATION D PRIVATE PLACEMENT OFFERINGS

The term "private placement" refers to the sale of a non-registered security. Private placements do not go through an underwriting process to meet the standards of public issue that the Securities and Exchange Commission (SEC) requires of public offerings. The investors in the placement, however, should be adequately accredited or sophisticated to understand and accept the risk that is assumed in a private placement. There is a certain degree of risk in the issue only for the fact that the SEC has not vetted the issue, in addition to normal business risks. Private placements also tend to be illiquid. Public offerings undergo a rigorous vetting process by the SEC. After the underwriting process, the public issue may be sold to the investing public. Public issues are usually viewed as less risky than private placements because of the SEC vetting and greater liquidity.

TOMBSTONE ADVERTISEMENTS

Tombstone advertisements are circulars advertising the impending new issue of the stock of a corporation. Tombstone advertisements are often thought of as a pre-prospectus advertisement, however, they are not considered an offer to buy or sell like the prospectus (this must be noted on the document). By definition, a tombstone advertisement is a one-page advertisement, whereas prospectuses are much longer and contain much more information. Tombstones also differ from prospectuses in that issuers are not required by law to provide a tombstone advertisement as they are a prospectus. The tombstone advertisement may contain as little information as the issuer likes, but it must contain no more than the name of the firm issuing the security, the type of security being issued, the quantity of the offering, the suspected initial price of the security, and the names of the underwriting syndicate.

FINRA RULE 5130

FINRA Rule 5130 was established to ensure that initial public offerings (IPO) are executed on a fair and unbiased basis. Rule 5130 applies to new issues, and its goals are to ensure that members do not keep a portion of the IPO for themselves or others that might entice them to and to prevent insiders from taking advantage of a new issue that retail investors may not have the same insight into. FINRA Rule 5130 established a list of persons prohibited from buying new issues. This list includes members of FINRA and their employees, representatives of the underwriters that underwrote the new issue, a shareholder that owns more the 10 percent of a FINRA member firm, portfolio managers, and immediate family members of the preceding. Rule 5130 also prohibits "spinning," or the act of sending an unfair proportion of the IPO to a person that may be able to send business back.

PROSPECTUS DELIVERY REQUIREMENTS IN THE SECONDARY MARKET

After an issuer has made an initial public offering (IPO) of its securities, it must make its prospectus available to retail buyers for a certain period of time. Because mutual funds are in a constant state of IPO, each time a customer purchases a new mutual fund, he must be provided with the prospectus. For securities that are traded over-the-counter (OTC) on the Pink Sheets, the prospectus must be provided for 90 days after the IPO. If the security made its IPO on an exchange, the prospectus must be given for the following 25 days. In the case of additional issues, OTC Pink Sheet stock prospectuses should be available for 40 days, whereas exchange-listed offerings are only required to provide the prospectus to buyers in the primary market, and not thereafter.

ANTIDILUTION

The term "antidilution" refers to an individual purchasing shares of a position that he owns when new shares are issued so that his position in the holding is not diluted. For example, if a person owned 10 shares of a 100-share offering, and the issuer offered 100 more, that person would have the option of buying at least 10 additional shares to maintain his 10 percent position of ownership. Antidilution exemptions allow restricted individuals that already own stock in a company to

63

participate in the initial public offering (IPO) of that company to prevent their ownership from being diluted. The restricted person must have held the position for at least 12 months, the new purchase cannot increase the restricted person's ownership in the company, and the shares may not be sold for at least three months after the IPO.

CROSS ORDER RULE 76

The term "cross order" describes an occurrence in which an NYSE member receives a manual order (not automated) to buy a security at the same time and price that he or she receives an order to sell that same security. This applies to orders of at least 10,000 shares or $200,000. Once the order is received, "he or she shall offer such security at a price which is higher than his or her bid by the minimum variation permitted in such security before making a transaction with himself or herself." The trader does this by entering the order on their handheld device, and making the offer available to the other traders for at least 20 seconds. After the 20 seconds has expired, the trader is free to cross the orders, or execute both orders and receive due compensation from both sides of the transaction.

NYSE RULE 80B

Rule 80B was established by the NYSE to combat panic selling that can occur when there is a downtrend in the markets overall. Rule 80B applies specifically to the Dow Jones Industrial Average, or DJIA. Once the DJIA reaches certain levels of downtrend, Rule 80B establishes "circuit breakers" to prevent panicked mass selling. Once the circuit breakers are tripped, trading is halted for various periods of time dependent upon the level of the halt. Level I halts result from a 10 percent drop in the DJIA, Level II at 20 percent, and Level III at 30 percent. A Level I halt before 2 p.m. will result in a one-hour trading halt. After 2 p.m. it is a half-hour halt. A Level II halt before 1 p.m. will result in a two-hour halt, after 1 p.m. it will result in a one-hour halt, and if it occurs after 2 p.m., the market will close for the day. At any point if the DJIA experiences a Level III halt, the market will close for the remainder of the day.

AUCTION SECURITIES MARKETS

Auction securities markets are markets in which buyers and sellers offer competitive bids and offers simultaneously. When buyers and sellers reach consensus, they then execute the trade on the trading floor. This differs from over-the-counter markets, or OTC markets, wherein prices are negotiated. In an auction market, the trades will only execute when the buyer and seller place identical bids and offers. Auction markets are the most visible type of market that the general public associates with buying and selling securities. The most well-known examples of auction markets in the United States are the New York Stock Exchange (NYSE), the American Stock Exchange (ASE), and the Chicago Board of Options Exchange (CBOE).

OVER-THE-COUNTER MARKETS

Over-the-counter markets describe markets that trade secondary market securities directly between parties, or "over-the-counter," without the supervision of an exchange, such as the New York Stock Exchange. Over-the-counter (OTC) markets differ from auction markets in that there is no bid/ask process as with auction markets. Buyers and sellers negotiate the market price of securities, and most orders are filled at the market price. Most buying and selling for retail investment customers happens in OTC markets, and the most well-known of all those markets in the NASDAQ Stock Market, or the National Association of Securities Dealers Automated Quotations. The NASDAQ has the second largest market capitalization in the world, while the New York Stock Exchange has the largest.

NASDAQ Stock Market

The NASDAQ began as a convenient means of monitoring stock quotes. It was an electronic quotation system and, due to the popularity and use of the electronic board, it became the world's first electronic trading system. The majority of over-the-counter trading that occurs for retail investors is executed via the NASDAQ. The NASDAQ provides an electronic communication network (ECN) to facilitate buyers and sellers that wish to communicate, and provides a system by which securities firms may list quotes and orders for the same security. This gives traders and investors looking for a certain security a convenient method by which they may find the best price for themselves or their customers, and provides a means by which to measure the volume of trading of NASDAQ listed securities.

Unlisted Trading Privileges

The term "unlisted trading privileges" refers to the privileges granted to members of the NASDAQ stock exchange concerning the trading of unlisted securities. Most exchanges have required minimums that must be met before they will list a security and make it available for trade. With the use of unlisted trading privileges, or UTPs, traders and investors have greater access to the capital markets if they wish to buy or sell a security that may have not met the minimum requirements of price and volume to be exchange listed. Exchanges that allow their members to trade UTP are under obligation of the SEC to monitor trades placed this way, and report activity in the UTP market to FINRA. The NASDAQ is not responsible for settling disputes about UTP transactions; the UTP exchange must find resolution to execution and trading issues.

Securities Markets

The four securities markets are simply named the first, second, third, and fourth markets. The first market is referred to as an auction market. First markets have actual trading floors where listed securities are traded. The second market is a negotiated market where unlisted securities trade over-the-counter, or OTC. The third market has been around since the 1970s, and was the initial market that presented actual competition for the first market. In the third market, listed securities are traded OTC, and the first market is bypassed because of the convenience of the third market. The fourth market is an OTC market that facilitates trading for securities (whether or not they are listed) amongst institutional investors. The fourth market is occasionally called the Electronic Communication Network, or ECN. Traders that make use of ECNs benefit from electronic systems that provide a constant stream of price and volume data regarding securities from other traders on the ECN.

MARGIN AGREEMENT

Before a broker/dealer is allowed to add margin features to a customer's account (and charge accordingly), the customer is required to sign a written margin agreement. Margin agreements will vary by broker/dealer, but each agreement must contain at least three sections. Each agreement should have a "credit agreement." A credit agreement describes to the customer how their variable interest rate will be used to figure the interest that the customer owes. By signing the "loan consent agreement," the customer agrees that the broker/dealer may loan to others (i.e., in the case of a short sale) the customer's securities that have been margined. Finally, all margin agreements will contain a "hypothecation agreement." The hypothecation agreement permits the broker/dealer to collateralize the securities in the client's account to cover their margin loan.

MONITORING MARGIN ACCOUNTS FOR PROPER HANDLING BY THE REGISTERED REPRESENTATIVES

Margin accounts are subject to many rules and regulations which may be unclear. It is the duty of the registered principal (RP) to assist registered representatives (RR) under their supervision in understanding and monitoring the accounts to ensure that the accounts comply with FINRA regulations, such as ensuring proper documentation is on file for the margin account. In addition to helping the RR stay compliant with FINRA and their customers, RPs should monitor margin accounts to ensure the RRs are not abusing the customer's account, whether intentionally or unintentionally. For example, if a customer is paying four percent interest to have a margin account, but it is totally invested in T-Bills that are paying .02 percent, then the customer is losing money and the RP should work with the RR to remedy this situation.

EX-DIVIDEND

There are several important dates that occur when an issuer declares a dividend. The first is the declaration date, in which the issuer announces the dividend. The next is the ex-dividend date, and the date of record (the date on which the investor must own the stock to receive the dividend). The ex-dividend date is the day after the last day that a buyer may purchase a stock and still receive the dividend. The ex-dividend date is one day before the date of record, because regular way settlement is T+2. When a transaction is said to be an ex-dividend transaction, it means that even if the buyer purchases the security before the payable date, he will not receive the dividend.

AFFIRMATIVE DETERMINATION

Affirmative determination describes the practice of registered representatives ensuring that their customers have custody of the securities that they have traded, and are able to deliver them in the normal settlement period (T+2). This conversation should be documented on the trade ticket. Affirmative determination

is in place to protect the buyer of the securities from unscrupulous sellers, but it also protects both the integrity of the stock market as a whole and the integrity of the broker/dealer through whom the transaction was effected. The most efficient method to meet affirmative determination is for the customer to hold their securities in street name so that the broker/dealer will have possession of the securities, and the customer will not have to prove custody of the securities.

NYSE RULES 410A AND 410B

Automated submission of trading data (NYSE Rule 410A) - a member is to transmit trade data in an automated format that is to include clearing house number, identifying symbol, date of execution, number of shares, transaction price, account number, and market center.

Reports of listed securities transactions effected off the Exchange (NYSE Rule 410B) - a member that has transacted a trade off of the Exchange is to report it to the exchange by the close of the next business day. The reports must contain information including time and date of transaction; stock symbol; number of shares; price; marketplace where transaction was executed; indication of whether it was buy, sell, or cross; whether transaction was executed as principal or agent; and contra side broker-dealer.

REPORTING TERMINATION

According to the NASDAQ Stock Market, the NASDAQ OMX BX, the NYSE MKT, and the NYSE Arca Rules, Form U-5 is to be used for a termination. It is to be submitted electronically, within 10 days of the termination. The member is to keep records of the filing for at least 3 years. Any necessary amendments are to be filed within 10 days of the event making the amendment required.

TRADES SUBJECT TO ADDITIONAL REVIEW

According to the NYSE MKT Rules, a member is—for trades subject to additional review—to either submit a written statement to the Exchange by the 15th of the month after the trade was completed, or if the trade is subject to an internal investigation that has not been resolved, make a written report to the Exchange detailing specific information.

DISCLOSURE OF SALES BY UNDERWRITING SYNDICATE MEMBERS

When syndicate members place orders for certain types of customers, they must disclose the sale. The accounts covered under this rule include accumulation accounts, a syndicate member's dealer account and/or any account related thereto, and any investment trust (municipal related) for which a syndicate member is responsible.

Supervise Communications with the Public

TELEPHONE CONSUMER PROTECTION ACT OF 1991

Registered representatives who desire to prospect for clients through telemarketing must follow regulations set forth by the Telephone Consumer Protection Act of 1991, or TCPA. These guidelines are as follows: calling individuals with whom the individual does not have a business relationship must be confined to the hours between 8 a.m. and 9 p.m. local time for the recipient of the call; the individual placing the call must identify himself and his firm and how he may be contacted and identify the purpose of the call; and, if the call recipient requests to be placed on a do-not-call list, the caller must comply. The do-not-call status must be maintained for five years. The TCPA applies to phone calls, fax machines and email, and these regulations must be applied to each method of communication.

SEMINARS AND PUBLIC PRESENTATIONS GIVEN TO THE GENERAL INVESTING PUBLIC

When a registered person speaks publicly to a group of potential customers, it is vital that their supervising registered principal approve the presentation beforehand. The Financial Industry Regulatory Authority, or FINRA, requires prior approval of presentations given at public appearances of registered individuals. It is the responsibility of the registered principal to train the registered individuals under their supervision to know the proper channels through which to go to facilitate public speaking engagements. FINRA requires the approval of such events as additional protection of non-sophisticated investors who may not understand what they hear, and are potential victims of misleading statements. After a registered principal approves a public event, he must maintain a log of public seminars and presentations given by registered representatives. The log must contain information as to what the seminar was about, the date and time of the event, and the name of the registered presenter.

FINRA RULE 2210

A qualified registered principal must approve all retail communication before its use or filing with FINRA, unless another member has already filed it and it has been approved and the member has not altered it. For institutional communications, members are to establish written procedures for review by a qualified registered principal of institutional communications. The procedures are to be designed to ensure that institutional communications company with the standards. All communications, retail and institutional, are to be retained according to requirements, and must include:

- a copy of the communication
- the name of any registered principal approving of the communication
- if not approved by a registered principal prior to first use, the name of the person who prepared it
- information about the source of information used in graphic illustrations
- if approval is not required for retail communication, the name of the member that filed it with FINRA, as well as the letter from FINRA

RULE 472

ADVERTISING

An advertisement is any communication that is published or used in print, electronic or other public media. This public media includes newspapers, periodicals, magazines, radio, television, telephone recordings, web sites, motion pictures, audio and video devices, telecommunications devices, billboards and signs. All advertisements must be approved prior to use by an allied member, supervisory analyst or other person described in Rule 342(b)(1), as long as this person is not the preparer of the advertisement. An advertisement that is for a public offering of a security must comply with the registration requirement of the Securities Act of 1933. The name of the member firm must appear in all advertisements, excluding recruitment advertisements.

MARKET LETTER

A market letter is a written comment on the condition of the market. Market letters may also recommend specific securities as long as they comply with the standards of Rule 472(j). The amount of information contained in a market letter is limited and supporting information must be offered. Market letters may include follow-ups to research reports and articles written by the member firm that are published in magazines. Market letters are generally limited to one page. Market letters must be approved in advance of their distribution. This approval may be given by an allied member, supervisory analyst or person designated under Rule 342(b)(1). The person who prepared the market letter may not give the approval.

SALES LITERATURE

Sales literature is any written or electronic material that discusses or promotes the products, services and facilities offered by the member firm or its personnel. Sales literature may also be a telemarketing script. Sales literature may include a discussion of how an investment may fit into an individual's financial plan. Sales literature may also include references to market letters, research reports, brochures or other communications published by the member firm. This approval may be given by an allied member, supervisory analyst or person designated under Rule 342(b)(1). The person who prepared the sales literature may not give the approval.

PUBLIC APPEARANCE

A public appearance is any participation by a member firm, its allied members or employees in a seminar, public forum, interactive electronic forum, radio or television interview or other public speaking appearance where the research analyst makes a recommendation or offers an opinion on an equity security. These public appearances must be approved in advance of publication or broadcast. This approval may be given by an allied member, supervisory analyst or person designated under Rule 342(b)(1). In addition, the member firm must set written supervisory procedures for allied members and employees who make public appearances.

RESEARCH REPORT

A research report is a written or electronic communication that includes an analysis of equity securities, individual companies or industries. The information included in the research report should be complete and sufficient enough to base an investment decision. If there is a question as to whether a document is a research report or a market letter, the document should be treated as a research report. Research reports must be approved by a qualified supervisory analyst. If the supervisory analyst does not have the technical expertise in a particular product area, the analysis contained in the research report may be co-approved by a product specialist of the member firm.

CORRESPONDENCE AND GROUP CORRESPONDENCE

Correspondence is the direct communication (including electronic communication) of a registered individual with an individual client. Group correspondence is defined as the same communication (i.e., form letters) sent to more than one but less than 25 individuals. FINRA firms do not need to approve correspondence or group correspondence to be compliant with FINRA regulations. However, if the FINRA member elects to not require that a registered principal, or RP, approve the correspondence, they must provide their employees with a clear written policy and implement a training program that educates their employees on proper correspondence with clients. Written proof of training must be maintained. Firms must also maintain three years of written correspondence for review should it need to be reviewed by a regulatory agency.

SALES LITERATURE AND ADVERTISEMENTS

Sales literature is defined as communication (electronic or otherwise) to greater than 25 individuals that is not communicated using mass media. Such communications include direct communication with the individuals via mail or email, usually as a form letter with some presentation of facts as an inducement to buy a product. Advertisements are any form of communication with the general public that are communicated via mass media such as the Internet, television, radio, newspaper, and all other forms of mass media. For a registered individual to use sales literature or an advertisement, it must first be approved by a registered principal, or RP. The sales material must then be filed with FINRA or a registered securities exchange at least 10 days prior to use.

SALES MATERIALS THAT DO NOT REQUIRE FILING WITH FINRA

Internal sales material and sales material distributed to institutional investors are not subject to FINRA's filing requirements. To be considered internal sales material, the material must only be distributed to other members and associates of members of FINRA. An example of this is a flyer that an investment company may provide to a registered representative advertising a product. Much of this material is considered for "advisers only" and not for use with the general public. Because institutional investors are considered sophisticated (thus not needing protection by FINRA), FINRA does not deem it necessary to review sales material provided to them. Internal and institutional sales material should be treated similarly to correspondence: it does not need to be filed with FINRA, but it should be retained for review by a registered principal. Additionally, if the creator of the materials has reason to believe that the end destination will be the general investing public, it should be treated as sales material and obtain pre-approval.

ECN

An electronic communication network, or ECN, is a system by which securities orders are matched to bypass the need for a third party. The matching is performed electronically, and allows buyers and sellers of securities to communicate directly without the need for a third party to facilitate their trading. ECNs must register with the Securities and Exchange Commission (SEC) as a broker/dealer, and collect a fee for their services. ECNs facilitate trading by displaying the optimal bid/ask prices for the same securities, and then automatically execute the transaction on behalf of the buyers and sellers. ECNs greatly reduce the time it takes to match orders for buyers and sellers. In addition to serving retail investors, ECNs also facilitate trading for institutional investors.

REQUIREMENTS FOR ADVERTISEMENTS, EDUCATIONAL MATERIALS, AND SALES LITERATURE RELATING TO OPTIONS TRADING

FINRA requires that each of its member firms that create advertisements, educational materials, and sales literature pertaining to options establish written policies regarding these advertisements, and that a registered options principal approve the written policy and approve literature created under the policy. In developing these written policies, many FINRA members over-comply to help prevent FINRA violations from ever occurring. The written policy should require that each piece of literature created discloses the special risks inherent with options investing, and that options investing consists of complex strategies that may not be suitable for all investors. When the advertisement makes a claim of potential gains associated with options investing, it should also be plainly stated that there are risks associated therewith as well. The guarantee of a liquid market by which an option may be closed should not be made. Finally, it should not be implied that options investing is suitable for all investors.

Series 9

Supervise the Opening and Maintenance of Customer Options Accounts

REVIEWING ACCOUNT SUITABILITY REGARDING OPTIONS INVESTING

The risks and reasons for investing in options varies widely by option type. While one type of options can find a place in every strategy, not all options are suitable for all strategies. It is very important for registered principals to monitor and train the registered representatives under their supervision to ensure that suitability for each options transaction is met. The most conservative investors may benefit from the income generated by writing covered calls. The same investor would be misadvised in selling an uncovered (or naked) call, or spending income by paying large premiums associated with complex options strategies. Conversely, an aggressive investor seeking large growth may not be suited to covered-call writing as it may only produce small amounts of income.

MARGIN REQUIREMENTS ASSOCIATED WITH UNCOVERED (OR NAKED) OPTIONS

When investors write uncovered options, they are potentially taking on an unlimited amount of risk. In the case of naked calls, the value of the underlying asset does not have a limit on how much the price may increase. Thus, the potential loss is limitless. In the case of naked puts, the loss is limited to the difference in the strike price and zero multiplied by the number of shares the put contracts cover. This is also a potentially large number. Because the potential for loss is so high in both cases, they may only be written in accounts with margin features that are governed by Regulation T. Regulation T does not allow the entirety of the position to be covered by margin. The customer must have cash in the account equaling the current premium receivable for the option and a specified percentage of the total value of the underlying holdings (20 percent for listed stocks) minus the amount of the option that has no intrinsic value.

REQUIREMENTS FOR UNCOVERED OPTIONS

Writers of uncovered options are subject to the same Regulation-T rules as those who purchase securities on margin in regards to the initial equity requirement and the minimum maintenance requirement. In addition to these requirements, the investor must also have cash in the account that is the sum of the current premium of the option and a specified percentage of the total value of the stock on which the option is written, but minus the amount of the option that is considered out-of-the-money. Investors may exclude the out-of-the-money portion because it is not in immediate danger of being exercised. Typically, firms who are members of self-regulatory organizations (SRO) require higher standards of compliance than the SRO of which they are members. This is to ensure that the firm does not come close to violating SRO standards and services the customer as thoroughly as possible.

72

APPROVAL PROCESS FOR DISCRETIONARY OPTIONS ACCOUNTS

For a client to open a discretionary options trading account (one in which a registered representative may transact on his behalf without prior approval), he must submit a new account application, an options trading agreement, and a written limited power of attorney to provide his representative with the authority to transact on his behalf. After these documents are submitted, the discretionary account must then be approved by the registered options principal (ROP) or sales supervisor. When discretionary orders pertaining to options are placed, they must be noted on the trade ticket as such, and the supervising ROP must approve the transaction on the trade by initialing the trade ticket.

FINRA RULE 2360

FINRA Rule 2360 requires members to keep a central file at their principal place of business to log complaints. The central file should make it easy to identify and retrieve information concerning complaints. This central file should at least include the identity of the complainant, the date that the firm received the complaint, the registered person servicing the account, a description of the complaint, and a record of the action taken by the member to resolve the complaint. The rule further goes on to require that the firm retain the options trading agreement at both the servicing branch and the OSJ branch. Additionally, statements must be maintained at both locations for at least six months, unless easily accessible (i.e., electronically stored), in which case statements need only be stored in one location.

FINRA RULE 2360(B) (12)

FINRA Rule 2360(b) (12) requires that each FINRA member submit a confirmation of transaction to its customers that buy or sell options. The following information is required to be on the confirmations sent to the customer: the type of option, the underlying security or index, the expiration month, the exercise price, the number of option contracts, the premium, the commission, the trade and settlement dates, whether it was a purchase or a sale transaction, whether it was an opening or a closing transaction, and whether the transaction was placed in a principal or agency capacity. The rule further requires that the options symbols distinguish exchange listed options from other transactions.

FINRA RULE 2360(B) (15)

FINRA Rule 2360(b) (15) requires that each FINRA member send statements of account monthly to each of their customers that open or change security or cash positions, other entries, interest charges, and other charges pertaining to options contracts. The preceding information should also be shown on each statement. If the customer's account does not have a transaction, but has an open options position or cash in the account, they should receive statements quarterly. The rule also requires that the statements of customers with margin accounts should show the marked-to-market price and value of the positions in the account, any outstanding balances in the account, and the account equity. Lastly, the statement should list any commissions charged and instructions for the customer to immediately notify the member of any discrepancies in the account.

DAY TRADERS

The term "day trader" refers to a trader that trades in securities in hopes of gaining intraday capital gains. To make day trading viable, the trader must have access to large amounts of capital. Occasionally this is accomplished with the assistance of margin accounts. FINRA requires day traders to keep at least $25,000 (or 25 percent of the margin value, whichever is greater) in equity in their day trading account, whereas regular margin accounts must only maintain 25 percent. Additionally, day traders benefit from greater purchasing power than regular retail margin accounts. Whereas typical margin accounts may use double the value of their special memorandum account for purchases, day traders may use quadruple the value of their special memorandum account for purchases. Lastly, FINRA prohibits day traders from benefiting from certain account guarantees that other accounts may access freely.

MAINTENANCE OF RECORDS OF OPTIONS COMPLAINTS AND TIMEFRAME TO FILE COMPLAINTS

FINRA requires that members segregate complaints regarding options from complaints regarding other securities transactions, and to keep a "current... separate central log... through which these complaints can easily be identified and retrieved." In addition to the branch in which the central log is maintained, records of options-related complaints must be maintained at the branch that is subject to the complaint. The information that must be maintained is the name of the person filing the complaint, date of the complaint, the registered person that is the object of the complaint, description of the complaint, and what action was taken. When a FINRA member receives an options-related complaint, the complaint should be forwarded within 30 days of receipt, instead of within 15 days of quarter end, as with other complaints.

COST BASIS AND WASH SALES

Cost basis is the amount of money an investor expends to open a position, in this instance an options position. The cost basis is used to determine whether an investor has a capital gain or a capital loss in the position when it is liquidated. If the cost basis is higher than the consideration received, it is a capital loss, and vice versa when money is made. The cost basis of a position is determined by adding the price of the open position to the fees incurred while opening the position. A wash sale occurs when an individual closes a position that has a capital loss (for the tax benefits), and reopens the position with the same or significantly identical holding within 30 days. When a wash sale occurs, the investor is not allowed to take the tax loss. The cost basis of an open option that an investor closes will determine the gain or loss, and thereby may limit the selections of new options to open with the proceeds.

SUPERVISING OPTIONS TRADING RELATED ACTIVITIES

The registered options principal, or ROP, is responsible for regularly monitoring options trading in customer accounts that fall under their jurisdiction and accounts for which their supervisees are responsible. ROPs should monitor computer-generated reports that flag suspicious or unusual activity. In the event that a customer may be acting of their own accord and possibly overreaching in their options-related activities, the ROP should ensure that someone reaches out to the customer and discusses their goals and activities with them. While supervising registered individuals, the ROP should check to ensure that recommended options trades are not only consistent with the customer's stated goals, but also suitable to their overall situation. For example, writing an uncovered call may provide a retiree with income, but it also puts them at risk for very large losses.

Margin Requirements for Writing Covered Options

Typically, when customers trade options in their accounts they do so using margin accounts. This is to provide liquidity to help them meet obligations associated with options that they might not otherwise be able to meet. Most firms require that accounts intended to allow certain types of options transaction be opened with margin features. However, when customers generate income by writing covered options, there is no risk that the customers will not be able to meet the obligations they may incur if their written options are exercised because they already own the position in a covered call, or have the cash to cover a put that they have written. If customers write a put and do not have all of the cash to cover that put, then they are required to have a margin account and meet margin requirements.

Margin Requirements for Accounts That Use Spread and Straddle Strategies

When investors use spread or straddle strategies in their accounts, they are required to have margin features added to that account. Concerning spread writing, the customer must have enough cash on deposit to cover a total loss on the option. For credit spreads, this is limited to the difference between the strike prices, and is often not very substantial. In the case of debit spreads, the loss is limited to the amount of premium the investor paid for the options. Customers are always long in the case of straddle options strategies, so the maximum loss and thereby maximum margin requirement equals the total of the premiums paid for the two open options, and the margin requirement is not subject to increase (or decrease) in the event of price movement of the underlying security.

Calculating Margin Requirements on Listed Securities

The margin requirement for listed equities is calculated as follows: the entirety of the current premium is added to 20 percent of the total market value of the underlying stock and then the out-of-the-money portion is subtracted from this total. As an equation it could be expressed as *Premium + 20percent of the stock's market value – out-of-the-money portion = required margin.* The out-of-the-money portion is subtracted due to its lack of value. Because the prices of securities fluctuate on a daily basis, the options in the margin account must be marked to market to reflect the current price of the underlying security. Thus, the required margin changes daily as the middle numbers of the equation fluctuates due to normal market movements.

REVIEW AND RETENTION OF CUSTOMER CORRESPONDENCE RELATED TO OPTIONS

The term "correspondence" refers to written communication with 25 or fewer customers. FINRA member firms are required to have a written policy regarding correspondence. FINRA does not require correspondence to be approved before it is distributed, but many firms implement an approval prior to the distribution process in order to prevent FINRA violations. For those firms that do not require principal pre-approval of options-related correspondence, they are under onus to properly and adequately train their employees in the proper use of language of correspondence. All correspondence from FINRA members must be maintained for review for at least three years after it is first distributed. These records must contain the name(s) of the person(s) preparing and distributing it, and the name of the reviewing registered options principal.

TIME LIMITATIONS ASSOCIATED WITH TRADING OPTIONS

Options are traded on exchanges during normal market hours, which are between 9:30 a.m. and 4:00 p.m., Eastern Standard Time. At the close of business on the third Friday of the month that a certain option expires, the option may no longer be traded. By 5:30 p.m. the same evening, any party holding an option loses the right to exercise the option, and at midnight of the Saturday night/Sunday morning immediately after the third Friday of the month, the options technically expire. The downtime between the cease of activity regarding the options and expiration provide options broker/dealers time to file all transaction with the Options Clearing Corporation.

Supervise Sales Practices and General Options Trading Activities

OPTIONS

Options are securitized contracts based on an underlying security, currency, or index. Dependent upon the option type, options give the buyer the right (but not obligation) to buy or sell a security at a set price or strike price within a certain period of time. The seller of the option receives a premium for taking the risk of creating the option and potentially having to buy or sell the underlying security for more or less than is optimal. The two basic options are calls and puts. The more complex options, such as straddles and spreads, are some combination calls and puts. Options allow investors to speculate on price movement of securities without having to commit capital to do so. They can also provide a source of income to the person writing (selling) the options.

CALL OPTIONS

A call option is the right (but not obligation) to buy a security at set price (or strike price) at some date in the future (subject to expiration). The writer, or seller, of a call option must make good on the promise (either by delivering the securities from the inventory or purchasing and delivering the securities) if the option is exercised. Call options are used by speculators who think that a stock will increase, but do not wish to expend capital on the position. Additionally, if a call is covered (the seller has the stock in their inventory), calls can be a safe income generator because the writer receives the premium, and only risks having to sell their stock at a price below market. Naked or uncovered calls (seller does not own the position) theoretically have unlimited risk, as the rise in the underlying stock is potentially limitless.

PUT OPTIONS

A put option is the right to sell a stock at a set price (or strike price) at some date in the future subject to expiration. The writer, or seller, of a put option must make good on his or her promise to buy the securities at the strike price regardless of the market price if the option is exercised. Put options may be used by speculators who hypothesize that the price of security may decrease, and want to benefit from that without opening a short position. Put option writers also benefit from premiums received when they sell the option, but it is generally not considered as attractive an option for generating income as is writing covered calls.

BROAD-BASED INDICES AND NARROW-BASED INDICES

Broad-based indices, sometimes called market indices, are a measurement of the composite value of a large index of stocks. Stocks selected within broad-based indices are usually placed there because they have a high correlation to other stocks and present a relatively accurate view of the market overall. The idea is that when the stock market decreases or increases, the index will move correspondingly. Narrow-based indices, also called industry indices, however, only base their index on a much smaller group of stocks that come from the same industry. Narrow-based indices are designed to provide a more accurate picture of a single industry than the market as a whole. Stocks in narrow-based indices tend to be highly correlated with each other, but not other stocks outside their industry.

MARKET RISK WHEN USING NARROW-BASED INDICES OPTIONS

Market risk, in general, describes the risk that the market as a whole will move in a downward direction. If a country has a strong economy, market risk is relatively low. Conversely, markets in a country that is in recession have high market risk.

Investors that decide to purchase narrow-based indices can be affected by market risk, and need to view it from multiple perspectives. For narrow-based indices investors, market risk can be mitigated by investing in staples such as energy and food. High market risk can present an opportunity for the investor to buy puts on the sector they think will be mostly negatively affected, and vice versa in markets with low amounts of risk.

AMERICAN-STYLE OPTIONS SETTLEMENT AND EUROPEAN-STYLE OPTIONS SETTLEMENT

American-style options settlement is the method by which options on individual equities are settled. They may be exercised any time before the option's date of expiration. By contrast, European-style options settlement is used to settle options written on indices and may not be exercised until the date of expiration. To further differentiate the two, investors do not actually receive shares of an index when their options expire (because it is not possible). Index options holders will receive the intrinsic value of their position at expiration if the option is in the money. By contrast, American-style options allow for a holder to receive shares of the underlying asset of the option. This is possible because holding individual shares is possible, where holding individual shares of indices is not.

IN-THE-MONEY, AT-THE-MONEY, AND OUT-OF-THE-MONEY OPTIONS

The phrases ending in "the-money" describe the position of an option as it approaches the strike price of the contract. Depending on the type of contract, the phrase "in-the-money" describes an option in which the price of a security has moved past the strike price, and the option may be exercised for a profit. The phrase "out-of-the-money" describes a security price that has moved past the strike price such that the option has no value. The phrase "at-the-money" describes a security price that matches the strike price of an options contract, and at any point following the strike price it would make sense to exercise an option. For example, the holder of a call option with a strike price of $35 on ABC stock would be out-of-the-money when the price of ABC reached $34, at-the-money at $35, and in-the-money at $36 (depending on the premium they paid).

CONCEPTS OF PARITY AND TIME VALUE RELATED TO STOCK OPTIONS

The time value of a stock option is a function of the amount of time left before an option expires. The value of an option is derived from the intrinsic value of the option and the time left until expiration. At the expiration date of the option, the time value of the option is zero. If there is intrinsic value left in the option and the time value is zero, then the option is considered to be at parity. The reason the term "parity" is applied in this case is because the intrinsic value of the option is equal to the market price of the underlying security.

FOREIGN CURRENCY OPTIONS

Foreign currency options allow investors to speculate on the movement of currency values. Foreign currency options (FCOs) settle European style because there are no shares to change hands. Contract sizes vary by the country issuing the currency, but most contract sizes are 10,000 per currency with the notable exception of 1 million Japanese yen. Contract premiums are quoted in $100 increments per point. FCOs expire on the Saturday following the third Friday of the month. The most common use of FCOs is for the hedging of currency risk by companies that do business internationally. The movement of currency can hurt the overall profit of a business transaction, so some companies buy foreign currency options to help cover some of the loss if the currency values move against them.

SPREAD AND STRADDLE OPTIONS STRATEGIES AND ASSOCIATED BULLISH/BEARISH STRATEGIES

Option spreads consist of investors buying calls or puts on a position and selling the same option with a difference as to expiration, strike price, or both. Depending upon their bull/bear outlook, this allows them to speculate on the movement of a security and have downside protection. Option straddles consist of the investor buying (or selling) both opposite options on the same underlying security. This is done when the investor thinks that the underlying holding will experience volatility, but they are not sure in which direction. Spreads use the same options, while straddles use opposite options. An investor using long call and short put spreads has a bullish outlook, while one using long put and short call spreads is considered bearish. Options investors using straddles anticipate volatility, and are neither bullish nor bearish.

CALCULATION OF THE BREAKEVEN POINTS FOR LONG AND SHORT STRADDLES

Because straddles utilize both calls and puts, the strategy has two different breakeven points for both long and short straddles. In the case of long straddles, the breakeven points are calculated by totaling the premium paid for both options, and then subtracting the premium paid from profit earned when the stock moves beyond the call strike price or below the put strike price. Once the profit equals zero (meaning it is no longer negative) the long straddle has broken even. Short straddles break even when the price of the underlying security moves in either direction and decreases the profit from premiums received to zero. Short straddles are straddles sold; the seller does not want the security prices to move.

MINIMUM INFORMATION IN WRITTEN SUPERVISORY PROCEDURES FOR PROFESSIONALS SELLING OPTIONS

Written supervisory procedures should at a minimum provide for the retention of applicable customer documents such as the retention of at least six months of statements and the options agreement document. Additionally, the written procedures should account for the review of accounts to determine that suitability issues are addressed, such as what may happen if an option is exercised, whether the client understands and can meet tax obligations associated with options investing, and the understanding of the strategies being implemented. Lastly, the procedures should address the review of the amount of trading in the account and determine if the frequency is excessive, the trades fit the customer's goals, unauthorized trades have been executed, and compliance with regulations are met.

DOCUMENTS RELATED TO OPTIONS TRADING ACCOUNTS THAT MUST BE RETAINED BY THE FIRM

To assist the regulators in ensuring that FINRA member firms are in compliance with regulations, they require member firms that allow options trading to maintain certain documents and provide them to the regulators upon request. Member firms must make available to FINRA all compliance and procedures manuals from the last three years. Customer order tickets for options trades placed and order confirmations for options trades placed must be maintained for three years, and blotters that contain and organize orders must be kept for six years. Any complaint that a customer submits in writing must be maintained for four years. Statements of customer accounts must be retained for six years. Finally, all FINRA members must retain their original articles of incorporation for the entire existence of the company.

SPECIAL STATEMENTS PROVIDED TO UNCOVERED OPTIONS WRITERS

Because the loss that results from uncovered options writing is potentially unlimited, customers who open accounts in which uncovered option writing is allowed must be furnished with a special statement for uncovered option writers. All special statements must follow a format that is generally approved by the exchange on which the options are traded. At a minimum, the special statement must contain language that speaks about the potential for unlimited loss with uncovered calls and puts; that uncovered call and put writing should only be done by those who understand the risks and have the means to cover very large losses and meet margin requirements associated therewith; that uncovered combinations also contain limitless risk; that the lack of a secondary market could leave the writer without a choice to close the option before expiration or exercise; and the fact that American-style option writers may be exercised at any time, whereas European-style options may only exercise after expiration.

COMBINATION STRATEGY AND STRADDLE STRATEGY OF OPTIONS INVESTING

The term "combination" describes a certain strategy of options investing very similar to straddles. The term "straddle" refers to an options investor buying or selling both a call and a put on the same underlying asset. Similarly, combinations consist of the investor buying or selling both a call and put on the same underlying asset, but whereas the strike price and expiration date are the same for the call and put in a straddle strategy, the strike price and/or the expiration date differ on the call and put in the combination strategy. While the owner of the straddle will benefit if the price of the underlying asset moves in either direction more than the premium he or she paid, combination investors may have more insight as to the movement of a security, and thereby stand to make a higher profit using the combination strategy than the straddle strategy.

OPTIONS TRADING PROGRAMS

The term "options trading program" describes a strategy of using a series of options purchases and/or sales to meet a certain goal. Options trading programs can be used to meet goals from secure income to speculation. When a customer is enrolled in an options trading program, and the program uses discretionary options, the customer must be given a written explanation of the strategy. When options trading programs are included in sales literature, the literature must include the past combined performance of the options included, and if the options lack historical performance, the sales literature must disclose this fact. Also of importance for disclosure purposes are any assumptions that are made in illustrating an options trading program, such as an assumption that a written option will not be exercised.

CBOE RULES 4.11-4.12

To ensure fair and orderly markets, the Chicago Board of Options Exchange (CBOE) established Rule 4.11-4.12 in order to limit the position and the exercise of options. This is accomplished by preventing a single large option holder from causing a massive market movement by opening or closing an unusually large option position. The exercise and position limits vary by security, and as the market has become more transparent and the flow of information more liquid, the CBOE has increased the limits. Occasionally, when an investor uses options to hedge a position, the CBOE will not subject to the position limit set forth in CBOE Rule 4.11. It should be noted that the limits are not limits per account, and the registered principal should aggregate the investor's accounts when calculating position and exercise limits.

WAYS IN WHICH SPLITS AND DIVIDENDS ADJUST OPTIONS CONTRACTS

Because many of the underlying securities of options contracts may be subject to events such as dividends and stock splits, the options contracts written on the securities must also be adjusted when such an event occurs. Typically, when dividends are issued on stocks that underlie options contracts, there is no adjustment made to the contract (with exception of additional stock offered as a dividend). However, because stock splits and reverse splits dramatically affect the price of the underlying security, the options contracts must also reflect the split proportionately. A two-for-one split will cause the strike price to be divided by two and the number of calls to be multiplied by two. In this manner, parity between the original and new options prices will be maintained. Stock dividends are treated similarly; if the strike price is affected, the option must be adjusted to accurately reflect the value of the original option.

ELECTRONIC LIMIT ORDER BOOK FOR PLACING AND EXECUTING OPTIONS TRADES

The Chicago Board of Options Exchange and the New York Stock Exchange each have an electronic limit order book to facilitate the trade of options on their exchanges. The electronic book is a method of automatically pushing options orders from traders to a central record system that tracks orders and assists traders in filling those orders. If a trader so desires, an open order may be left on the book until some point at which it is filled. After orders that have been placed on the electronic book have been filled, the electronic book reports the details back to the broker/dealer that placed the order. As long as the options order is complete, there is no limit to the use of the electronic book other than the system's maximum storage capacity. The minimum order for the electronic book is one contract.

EXERCISING OPTIONS

When an option is in the money, the investor will usually either sell the option to another investor, or he or she will exercise the option. In the case of exercising call options, the investor will pay another investor the amount of the strike price of the option per share and then receive the shares. If an investor exercises a long put, he will sell the stock to an options writer at the strike price of the option. Whenever the option is exercised, the exchange on which the option is traded will designate a firm that has sold the same option to fulfill the obligation, and the firm will select a customer who wrote the option to fill it. Exercise by exception occurs when an option expires, but is in the money. If an option is in the money at all when it expires, the Options Clearing Corporation will automatically exercise that option on behalf of the buyer.

DESIGNATING FIRMS TO FULFILL OPTIONS OBLIGATIONS

In the event that an option is exercised, the Options Clearing Corporation, or OCC, will randomly select a broker/dealer to fulfill that obligation. When the broker/dealer is chosen, the OCC will then designate a customer who has written the option to fulfill the obligation. This is known as assignment, and the writer is the assignee. Assignees are designated by one of two methods: random selection and first-in-first-out, or FIFO. While random selection is self-explanatory, FIFO means that the person who first wrote the option will be required to fill it first. If he or she did not write enough options to cover the assignment, then the next chronological option writer will be assigned as well. Customers must be notified in advance whether the allocation method is FIFO or random.

CBOE RULE 11.2

The Chicago Board of Options Exchange (CBOE) Rule 11.2 requires that all firms that trade in options establish a method by which customers are selected to fulfill obligations associated with options exercises. The rule specifically states that the method by which they are selected must be either "automated, random selection" or "first in, first out" (also referred to as the FIFO method). The options trading firm must report its method of selection to the CBOE, and may not change the method unless it is reported to and is approved by the CBOE or another self-regulatory organization (SRO). Each options trading firm must also keep three years of documentation proving which method was selected, and that that method is still in use.

CBOE RULE 11.3

Chicago Board of Options Exchange (CBOE) Rule 11.3 dictates that "Delivery of the underlying security upon the exercise of an option contract... shall be in accordance with the Rule of the Clearing Corporation." This rule was established to prevent abuse by options writers in the event they cannot or refuse to deliver the security upon which an option was based. CBOE Rule 11.3 further goes on to describe the time limit for delivery of cash or delivery of securities (whichever the option contract requires) as "as promptly as possible after the exercise of an option contract by a customer." Generally, the language regarding the clearing corporation and the "promptly" admonition indicates that the delivery of securities should be as if they were purchased on an exchange.

OFF-EXCHANGE TRANSACTING AND REPORTING

New York Stock Exchange (NYSE) Rule 756 expressly forbids off-exchange trading if the premium given for a transaction exceeds one dollar, or unless the best execution for the customer is not on the exchange. The one-dollar nominal premium allows for accommodation liquidations of worthless options for tax reporting and paper trails. The NYSE requires that any person who executes an options trade-off exchange record information surrounding the transaction such as the date, time, the customer for whom the trade was executed, and the customer's account number. The broker/dealer that performed the trade is then required to maintain these records for a minimum of three years. Options trades affected through the NASDAQ trading system are specifically excluded from the prohibitions set for in NYSE Rule 756.

SPECIAL CONSIDERATIONS WHEN EXERCISING AN OPTION PRIOR TO A DIVIDEND BEING PAID ON THE UNDERLYING STOCK

Some investors holding in-the-money options may be waiting for the optimal time to exercise the option. For some, the declaration of a dividend on the underlying stock on which the option is written may provide the opportunity for which they are looking. The investor exercising the option to receive the dividend, however, should carefully consider the dates surrounding the issue of the dividend. Exercising an option and buying the stock as a result of exercise can take longer than the traditional T+2 for the stock underlying the option to settle. Thus, if the investor exercises the trade the day before the ex-dividend date, the security will likely not have settled in his account by the date of record that would have entitled him to receive the dividend he sought

Supervise Options Communications

APPROVAL REQUIREMENTS FOR COMMUNICATION WITH RETAIL CUSTOMERS

When registered individuals desire to communicate with the investing public, the communication must first be approved by a registered options principal, or ROP, and then the ROP must file the communication with FINRA. FINRA requires that the communication be filed at least 10 days before it is first used. It is important to note that filing with FINRA does not indicate FINRA's approval of the communication; it must still be approved by FINRA before use. In the event that FINRA reviews and rejects the piece, it may not be used. However, if an edited version is submitted and not rejected, then it may be used. Any retail investor communication that FINRA approves is not required to have the approval of the registered options principal (i.e., a previously rejected piece that has been approved after edits).

INCLUDING PERFORMANCE PROJECTION OF OPTIONS IN CUSTOMER COMMUNICATIONS

FINRA members are permitted to project performance of options in sales literature based on their historical performance as long as certain disclosures are made along with the advertisement and potentially misleading language is omitted. The literature must indicate that past performance does not guarantee future performance, and the numbers used in the projection must be clearly established. Costs related to options strategies must be disclosed and assumptions made must be acknowledged. Any projection of future performance must be reasonable based on past returns and current market conditions. Any risks inherent to the strategy must be plainly disclosed. If annual rates of return are used in the literature, the numbers must be reinforced with at least 60 days of data used to calculate the annualization, and formulas used to make projections must be listed in the literature. Finally, the literature must clearly claim that the projection may be attained only if the variables in the strategy are identical to those of the historical calculations.

REQUIREMENTS FOR FINRA MEMBERS USING PAST PERFORMANCE INDICATORS IN SALES LITERATURE

FINRA permits its members to use the past performance of options in sales literature based on their historical performance as long as certain disclosures are included in the advertisement and potentially misleading language is omitted. The information shown must be presented in a fair and balanced manor, and not just include profitable options trades that were made during the time period, but reasonably similar options trades that may have incurred losses as well. The literature must also include the date, time, and price of each opening and of each closing transaction. The literature may contain an average of the preceding information instead as long as the size of the contracts and the strategy concerning the treatment of the contracts are disclosed. All costs associated with the strategy must be disclosed, such as interest charges or commission received. Additionally, a fair representation of the performance of the market as a whole should be included. Lastly, the literature should clearly indicate that past performance does not guarantee future results.

OPTIONS COMMUNICATIONS WITH THE PUBLIC

Rule 2220 defines three types of options communications with the public:

- Advertisements are directed at a mass audience using a public media such as newspaper, magazine, radio, television, film, video and billboard. Advertisements are not required to be accompanied or preceded by an option disclosure statement.
- Educational material is provided to customers or the public. The purpose of educational material is to explain the nature of standardized options markets or options strategies.
- Sales literature is a written communication distributed to customers or the public. Sales literature contains analysis, performance reports, projections or recommendations regarding options. Information communicated during seminars and lectures that pertains to options is also considered sales literature.

Supervise Associated Persons and Personnel Management Activities

BREAKEVEN POINT AND INTRINSIC VALUE OF OPTIONS

The term "breakeven point" describes the position of an option when the value of the underlying holding has exceeded the strike price such that the increase in value of the option exceeds the premium the purchaser paid for the security. For example, if a purchaser paid $100 for an option to buy 100 shares of ABC stock, the breakeven point would be at the point that the value of the option exceeded the price paid for it by $100. The intrinsic value of an option is the difference in the value of an option and the strike price. Options do not have negative intrinsic value; they are considered worthless while the calculated value of intrinsic value is negative. Once the value of an option passes the breakeven point, it is considered to have intrinsic value for the holder. Any option that is in-the-money has intrinsic value and may be traded as a security, but it may not necessarily have reached breakeven until the stock price exceeds strike price plus premium paid.

TRADING ROTATIONS

Trading rotations occur at the beginning of options trading each day when the exchange opens. The designated primary market maker in each security will request bids and/or offers from the trading floor to begin the initial price quotes on the options. This is known as the opening rotation. Quotes on options that expire the soonest will be established first, and the process will continue with the next soonest expiration date until all quotes are published. Only after the opening prices are established will trading begin. Closing rotations are executed on the third Friday of each month (assisting traders in the closing of options for which they have orders); this process is also facilitated by a designated primary market maker. To expedite a potentially lengthy process in opening and closing rotations, the CBOE established the Rapid Opening System to automate the process of trading rotation and facilitate "fast markets."

TRADING HALTS

The following are FINRA rules regarding trading halts:

- Prohibition on transactions, publication of quotations, or publication of indications of interest during trading halts (FINRA Rule 5260) - if trading is halted for a specific security, no trading activities can be made on the security.
- Trading halts (FINRA Rule 6120) - FINRA will halt the trading of a security otherwise than on an exchange in certain situations when the market in power calls for a trading halt, or to permit dissemination of material news, obtain material information, obtain material information in the public interest. Other reasons include when extraordinary market activity is occurring.
- Trading halts due to extraordinary market volatility (FINRA Rule 6121) - FINRA will halt all trading activity otherwise than on an exchange in any stock if other major securities markets have done the same in response to extraordinary market volatility, or if directed by the SEC.

ORDER OF PRIORITY FOR OPTIONS ORDERS

The normal order of priority for options trades is to execute the trades that have the soonest expiration dates first. This ensures an efficient and fair environment in which to trade options because the most urgent requests are filled soonest. Options spread strategies are the exception to this rule. In the event that an investor places a spread option trade, due to the dual option nature, the spread order is given priority over other single options contracts that may have normally been afforded a higher priority in the order chain. This helps spread option traders execute their desired strategy by possibly preventing the absence of options that are vital to their strategy.

85

CABINET TRADING

Cabinet trades are used by options investors to close an option position that has no value prior to the expiration date. Cabinet options trades are executed at one dollar for each contract, and must be submitted in writing to the market maker who then executes the cabinet trades in the order in which he or she received the orders. The one-dollar execution price is nominally zero for tax reporting purposes, and the sale generates a paper trail that assists auditors and investors both in tracking options on which they may have lost money; this has led to them being referred to by some as accommodation liquidations. Because cabinet trades are executed on worthless securities, they are not reported on tickers, as this may induce synthetic market movement. They are, however, still reported to the governing exchange.

FLOOR BROKERS

Floor brokers are members of trading floors that accept options orders from CBOE member firms. They execute trades from all participants on the trading floor and fill orders from the electronic book, but they are not allowed to trade in their personal accounts. Floor brokers can work in a self-employed capacity and charge others fees for their services, or they may work for a CBOE member, often for a salary. Like registered representatives, it is the duty of the floor brokers to obtain the most optimal terms for their customers. To assist the floor broker in efficiently filling orders, they have time, price, and size discretion. This helps floor brokers execute the customers' requests in the most efficient manner, but they are not allowed discretion in other facets of options trades, such as the underlying security.

MARKET MAKERS

Market makers are responsible for providing liquidity on an exchange. Each market maker has a specific security or set of securities for which he or she is responsible to provide bids and offers for options on those securities. The most commonly traded options exchange is the Chicago Board of Options Exchange, or CBOE, so options market makers usually deal with other CBOE members. Options market makers are CBOE members that trade in a principal capacity (for their own account) and stand ready to fill orders when there is no demand from for an options trade from other CBOE members. Likewise, when another CBOE member wishes to buy an option and there are none available, the market maker will create an option for the participant to buy.

DESIGNATED PRIMARY MARKET MAKER

The designated primary market maker, or DPM, functions as both a market maker and a floor trader. The DPM is typically a Chicago Board of Options Exchange (CBOE) member that is responsible for making the market in a specific security. DPMs function as floor traders by filling orders from other floor traders, market makers, and the electronic book. Because DPMs function as both floor traders and market makers, they are not subject to the same limitations as each individual role. DPMs are appointed by the CBOE to ensure that trading of options in their specified security or securities is efficient and equitable. It should be noted that any equity that has options based on it will have a DPM. DPMs are also responsible for executing trading rotations.

REQUIRED DUTIES OF REGISTERED PRINCIPALS WHO SUPERVISE OPTIONS TRADING

To ensure compliance with regulations and guarantee that the customer is being serviced properly, the registered options principal, or ROP, must monitor many aspects of the branches under their supervision. The more supervision there is, the less likely it becomes that a violation will occur. Nevertheless, at a minimum the ROP has to review and approve new accounts with option agreements, train the registered individuals under the ROP's supervision in the proper handling of options accounts, approve options related correspondence, audit options accounts with discretionary trading authority, check for suitability and potential violations (i.e., too frequent or too large transactions), ensure that the recommendations of those under their supervision is suitable, compel their supervisees to inform their customers of requirements related to margin investing, review forms for accuracy and compliance, ensure adherence to anti-money laundering procedures, and create written procedures for communications with the public.

DOCUMENTATION WHEN CUSTOMER OPENS ACCOUNT WITH INTENT TO TRADE OPTIONS

When customers open new accounts with intent to trade options in the account, they should complete a new account form as usual, but the servicing branch should also collect a signed options agreement from the customer. While the new account applications will contain the customers' basic personal data (name and address, among others), the options agreement expresses the customers' desire to trade options, their investment experience, the reason they wish to trade options, how they are employed, types of options they plan on writing or buying, the date that the options disclosure document was given, their annual income, net worth, liquid net worth, whether or not they are married and have dependents, whether they are of legal age, from where their background information was obtained, and the signatures of the registered individual who services the account and the supervisor who approved the account.

REVIEWING THE OPTIONS ACCOUNT AGREEMENT AND DELIVERING THE OPTIONS DISCLOSURE DOCUMENT

It is the duty of the registered options principal, or ROP, to review the new options account paperwork for accuracy and completeness. If part of the application is incomplete, then the options agreement is not valid and the firm is in violation of regulations if options are traded in the account. After the ROP reviews the documentation for completeness, he or she must then sign the account paperwork for approval of the account. Within 15 days of approving the account, the ROP must ensure that his supervisees verify the customer's identity and deliver the options disclosure document, or ODD. Options accounts are not in good order unless the ODD has been delivered at or prior to the options account being approved.

Series 9/10 Practice Test

1. A General Securities Sales Supervisor at a FINRA-registered firm must have all of the following except...

    a. Passed the Series 9/10 exam.
    b. Series 7 registration.
    c. Two years direct experience or three years related experience in the subject area to be supervised.
    d. A credible record.

2. Which of the following would disqualify a person from being registered under SRO rules?

    a. A felony conviction in the past 15 years
    b. A securities misdemeanor in the past 10 years
    c. Not completing required minimum training period at firm
    d. A person who has been out of the securities industry for longer than 1 year

3. Member organizations must investigate all but which of the following of personnel they intend to register?

    a. Good character
    b. Business reputation
    c. Criminal record
    d. Qualifications

4. True or False: Having a registered representative simultaneously carbon copy email the supervisor an email containing a sales piece to a prospect is an acceptable way to approve correspondence.

5. In the SEC's oversight of FINRA, which of the following actions are not specifically provided for in the Maloney act?

    a. The SEC can review FINRA disciplinary actions.
    b. The SEC can disapprove any FINRA rule.
    c. The SEC can bring suit against FINRA members for embezzlement or misappropriation of funds.
    d. The SEC can suspend or revoke FINRA registration for failure to enforce compliance with its rules.

6. Which of the following are NOT true of the cooling-off period of the registration process for new issues?

    a. Preliminary prospectus (red herring) is used
    b. No discussions with customers is allowed
    c. Cooling-off period is 20 days long
    d. No sales are allowed

7. Which of the following securities are exempt from registration and prospectus requirements of the 1933 Act?

    a. US government securities
    b. Municipal securities
    c. Securities issued by Savings and Loans
    d. Commercial paper maturing in 365 days or less
    e. All of the above

8. In a private placement of $1 million, which of the following investors are allowed to purchase securities?

    a. The CFO of the issuer
    b. A couple with a net worth of $5,000,000
    c. An individual with an income of $50,000 and a net worth of $500,000
    d. An insurance company
    e. All of the above

9. True or False: Under Rule 144A, the holding period is reduced from six months to 30 days for qualified institutional investors (at least $100 million invested in securities not affiliated with entity).

10. All of the following are pertinent aspects of the U4 except...

    a. Must be given to employee for review.
    b. Must include 10-year employment history.
    c. Must be retained for three years.
    d. Must indicate licenses held, including insurance and commodities.

11. In overseeing sales personnel, which of the following practices are not indicators of a lack of suitability for clients?

    a. Excessive turnover of the account
    b. Trading of mutual fund shares
    c. Consistent profits on low-priced stock trading
    d. Recommendations that represent a significant percentage of the customer's liquid assets

12. All of the following are required disclosures for analysts' research reports except...

    a. Current price of the security.
    b. Analyst ownership of equity in subject company if ownership is greater than one percent of outstanding equity.
    c. If the member firm makes a market in the subject security.
    d. If the member firm has received compensation from the issuer in the past 12 months.

13. A registered person's website can be subject to treatment as all of the following except...

    a. A public advertisement.
    b. Sales literature.
    c. A research report.
    d. Public communications, such as a seminar.

14. True or False: Only if all of the following conditions are met may a primary personal residence of an associated person be exempt from branch office registration...

    a. Only associated persons who are part of the same immediate family, and reside at the same place, may conduct business at the residence.
    b. The residence may not be represented as an office of the firm, nor may it be used to meet with customers.
    c. Customer funds and securities may not be handled at the residence.
    d. Electronic communications, including email, must be made through the firm's system.
    e. The firm must maintain a list of all residence locations.

15. Regarding the personal trading of analysts and members of their households, all of the following are true except...

    a. An analyst is not permitted to trade against his recommendations.
    b. Analysts are prohibited from buying or selling securities in companies regularly covered by that firm's analysts in 45 days before or five days after the publication of a report on subject company.
    c. Analysts must not buy or receive shares in a company in the same sector they cover prior to its IPO.
    d. An analyst may have a passive investment in a covered company where they are not making decisions or directing trades, as in through a mutual fund.

16. In disciplinary proceedings, a Hearing Panel can impose all of the following penalties except...

    a. Fine a member firm or associated person up to $1 million per infraction.
    b. Censure a member firm or associated person.
    c. Expel a member firm or cancel its membership.
    d. Impose any other fitting sanction.

17. Which of the following is considered a minor rule violation that is subject to different enforcement?

    a. Analyst front-running a security recommended in a firm research report
    b. Failure to file advertisements on time
    c. Failure to file timely reports of one percent positions
    d. Failure to submit timely Firm Element Continuing Education

18. Which of the following disputes does not have to be arbitrated?

a. Disputes involving members against other members
b. Disputes involving public customers against members
c. Disputes between members and the National Securities Clearing Corporation
d. Disputes involving employment discrimination between members and associated persons

19. A pre-dispute arbitration clause must be highlighted and must be followed by which of the following disclosures?

1. Arbitration is final and binding on all parties.
2. Typically the panel will include a majority of arbitrators who were or are affiliated with the securities industry.
3. Parties are waiving their right to seek remedies in court, including the right to a jury trial.
4. Parties' right to appeal or seek modification of rulings by arbitrators is strictly limited.

a. 1, 2, and 4
b. 2 and 3
c. 1, 3, and 4
d. 1, 2, 3, and 4

20. Which of the following requirements that must be satisfied to solicit a customer to purchase penny stocks prior to purchase is not correct?

a. Determine suitability of account
b. Deliver a written and signed statement to customer regarding the suitability determination
c. Obtain from customer a written agreement to the transaction indicating identity and quantity to be purchased
d. Requirements are waived for an established account (open for at least six months) and who have already effected three penny-stock transactions with the same broker

21. Which of the following transactions are subject to the penny stock disclosure rules?

a. Transactions with an institutional accredited investor
b. Solicited transactions that represent less than five percent of investors' liquid assets
c. Transactions with an officer, director, or five percent owner of the company
d. Private placements

22. If a person walks in off the street to open an account to buy stock, all of the following must be obtained before the transaction can occur except...

   a. Customer name and address.
   b. Customer social security number or tax ID number.
   c. Signature of the RR opening account.
   d. Signature of principal approving the account.
   e. All of the above.

23. Which of the following scenarios would be appropriate without prior written discretionary authority?

   a. Client leaves a voicemail for RR at 6:00 p.m. saying, "Please buy 100 shares ABC in the morning at a reasonable price."
   b. Client asks RR to buy some shares of XYZ, but doesn't specify how many shares or price.
   c. Client asks RR to buy 100 shares of BCD at a reasonable price before close of session today.
   d. Client asks RR to buy 100 shares of best utility stock for income today before market closes.

24. Which of the following is not an acceptable action performed by someone granted a durable power of attorney?

   a. To purchase or sell real estate
   b. Have owner of property declared incompetent
   c. Make legal claims or conduct litigation
   d. Donate money to charitable institutions

25. Which of the following investments makes it impermissible for a member firm to open an account and transact business with an employee of another member firm without fulfilling obligations under SRO rules?

   a. Only invests in preferred stocks
   b. Only invests in a variable annuity contract
   c. Only invests in unit investment trusts
   d. Only invests in redeemable investment company shares

26. The following are all characteristics of a custodial account except...

   a. Donor's gift of cash into account is irrevocable.
   b. Margin trading is not permitted.
   c. Custodian's tax ID number used until minor is age 14.
   d. Only one custodian and one minor per account.

27. In supervision of associated persons, in which of the following activities does an employee NOT have to report his participation?

  a. RR is helping to arrange a loan between a client and a local merchant.
  b. RR signed up to volunteer with local Big Brother, Big Sisters, a nonprofit 501c3 organization.
  c. RR has taken a part-time job on the side to help out with the family business.
  d. RR has invested in a cattle breeding venture.

28. Which of the following is NOT a special provision that must be followed when a BD member conducts business on the premises of a deposit-taking financial institution?

  a. The BD must clearly display its name in the area in which it conducts business.
  b. The disclosures Not FDIC insured, No Bank Guarantee, and May Lose Value must be used in all communications and on all signs.
  c. Where practical, the BD's activities should be conducted in a physically distinct location from the area where retail deposits are taken.
  d. When opening a customer account, disclosures must be given orally and in writing.

29. According to SRO rules, a member organization must report which of the following activities involving its members, allied members, or employees to FINRA once discovered?

  a. Any verbal complaint involving theft or misappropriation of funds
  b. Any arrest, arraignment, indictment, or conviction for any criminal offense
  c. Any activity in which they are named as a defendant or respondent in any proceeding brought by a regulatory organization alleging violation of federal securities laws
  d. Any expiration or non-renewal of registration by any securities, insurance, or commodities regulatory or self-regulatory organization

30. Which of the following needs to be held longer than two years?

  a. Institutional sales material and the name of the person who prepared it
  b. All electronic communications between representatives and clients or prospective clients
  c. Thank you notes, birthday cards, and other non-business correspondence
  d. All of the above

31. Under MSRB rules, concerning records of agency and principal transactions, which of the following is false?

  a. Records of agency and principal transactions must be segregated.
  b. All trade tickets must be retained for six years.
  c. If an agency order is cancelled, a record of the terms, conditions, dates and date of cancellation and, if possible, the time of cancellation are all required.
  d. All of the above.

32. Local Government Investment Pools (LGIPs) are permissible investment vehicles for which of the following?

    a. A local library
    b. Cities, towns, and counties
    c. A school district
    d. All of the above

33. True or False: Because the interest on contributions grows tax free, 529 prepaid tuition plans are considered to be municipal fund securities.

34. The following activities are duties of which person?

    Training of municipal securities principals or municipal securities representatives
    Underwriting, trading, or sales of municipal securities
    Any other acts which involve communication, directly or indirectly, with public investors in municipal securities

    a. Municipal securities sales principal
    b. Financial and operations principal
    c. Municipal securities representative
    d. Municipal securities principal

35. MSRB rules permit unregistered clerical personnel to read and transmit approved quotations in all of the following situations except...

    a. When specifically authorized in writing by client.
    b. When closely supervised by a duly qualified municipal personnel.
    c. When familiar with normal type and size of transactions effected for customer or account.
    d. When verbally authorized by client.

36. True or False: MSRB considers advertisements that only disclose yield to call (YTC) to be misleading.

37. An in the money call option's value is driven by which of the following factors?

    a. Volatility
    b. Time
    c. Intrinsic value
    d. All of the above

38. Which of the following is NOT true concerning the Options Clearing Corporation (OCC)?

    a. The OCC is regulated by the SEC.

    b. The OCC acts as a third party in all option transactions.

    c. The OCC has authority in approving a firm's option advertising and public communications.

    d. The OCC is owned proportionately by the exchanges where listed options trade.

39. Which of the following options are allowable to an investor who has sold a call option and is assigned an exercise notice?

    a. May instead close out the position by buying back the call on the same day of assignment.

    b. They must honor the exercise notice.

    c. They may pay cash in lieu of the stock position plus the value of the premium.

    d. May instead close out the position by buying back the call within two business days if still ahead of expiration date.

40. Which of the following options strategies would not be appropriate for an investor interested in income and preservation of capital?

    a. Selling covered calls

    b. Buying puts on owned long stock

    c. A cashless collar

    d. Uncovered put writing

41. An investor wanting to get a stock at a lower price than the current market could…

    a. Buy a call.

    b. Sell a call.

    c. Sell a put.

    d. Buy a put.

42. What is the best way to make money on a stock move, regardless of direction?

    a. A collar

    b. Short straddle

    c. Long straddle

    d. Short combination

43. A strategy where the investor buys a call and sells another call at a different strike price but the same expiration date on the same security is called a…

    a. Horizontal spread.

    b. Vertical spread.

    c. Diagonal spread.

    d. Calendar spread.

44. Which of these are appropriate strategies for an investor bullish on a particular stock?

    1. Net Debit Call spread
    2. Net Credit Put spread
    3. Net Credit Call spread
    4. Net Debit Put spread

    a. 1 and 3
    b. 2 and 4
    c. 1 and 2
    d. 3 and 4

45. True or False: A butterfly spread is essentially a volatility spread, designed to make money off large moves in any direction in the underlying security.

46. The following are all true of Long-Term Equity Options except...

    a. They are commonly known by the trade name LEAPS.
    b. Their maturities extend as long as 39 months.
    c. The CBOE lists LEAPS on the 500 stocks in the S&P 500 as well as 10 indexes.
    d. LEAPS use American style exercise, with delivery on the next business day after exercise.

47. Which of the following is NOT true of the VIX?

    a. The VIX has a European style exercise and settlement is in cash.
    b. The VIX is designed to reflect the view of expected stock market volatility over the next 60 days.
    c. The VIX is calculated using the S&P 500 Index option bid and ask quotes.
    d. The exercise settlement value is determined by a special opening equation and is quoted as VRO.

48. Which of the following is NOT true of the Interbank Market?

    a. The Interbank Market is not regulated or centralized in any location.
    b. The most common transactions are spot and forward transactions.
    c. The Interbank Market is where foreign exchange rates are established.
    d. Banks do not take positions for their own accounts, but act as brokers for other banks and commercial customers.

49. True or False: The opposite of a foreign currency purchase is a US dollar sale.

50. All of the following are characteristics of FLEX Options except...

    a. There is a continuous ready market for FLEX Options.
    b. Expiration may be up to three years for equity options.
    c. Criteria such as expiration date, strike price, and exercise style are flexible.
    d. There is no physical delivery upon exercise.

Answer Key and Explanations

1. C: The qualification is one year of direct experience or two years of related experience in the subject area to be supervised.

2. B: A felony conviction in the past 10 years would disqualify any candidate. SRO rules do not require a minimum training period, although many firms do. A person who has been out of the industry longer than two years must pass a qualifying exam before being qualified.

3. C: Criminal records will be investigated during the registration process through fingerprinting and background checks. Member firms must investigate the other aspects of individuals prior to beginning registration.

4. False: Email communications that are considered sales literature must be approved by a registered principal PRIOR to use.

5. C: This is not an authority specified in the Maloney Act, but the other three are.

6. B: Discussions with customers are allowed in the form of indications of interest, which are not binding.

7. D: Commercial paper is defined as maturing in 270 days or less and is exempt from registration requirements.

8. E: All of the above. If the placement offering was OVER $1 million then option C would not be allowed as he is not an accredited investor.

9. False: Under Rule 144A the holding period is eliminated completely, increasing liquidity in the marketplace for privately placed securities.

10. A: The U4 does not need to be given to the employee. The U5, upon termination, does need to be given to the employee.

11. C: Consistent profits on stock trading, even if they are in low-priced stocks, is not a sign of unsuitable investments. However, blanket recommendations of low-priced stocks to customers with limited resources and a preoccupation with quickly gaining huge profits can indeed be a sign of unsuitable activity.

12. B: Disclosure of ownership over one percent is related to the member firm, not the individual analyst. Analysts are also subject to SEC Regulation AC (Analyst Certification) where they must state that the report reflects their personal views and that no compensation has been received that is related to the specific recommendation in the report.

13. C: A website of a research report cannot be construed as an analyst's research report. All of the website can be considered an advertisement and as communication

97

with the public, and subject to all rules and regulations governing such. All websites must be approved by a registered principal prior to use.

14. True: If all of these and other conditions are met with, the residence may be exempted from branch office registration.

15. B: Analysts are prevented from buying securities 30 days before publication of a report, not 45 days.

16. A: A Hearing Panel can impose a fine on a member firm or associated person with no monetary limit.

17. B: Failure to file advertisements on time is one of the minor rule violations that can be handled with a different enforcement approach.

18. D: Claims alleging employment discrimination, including sexual harassment, do not require arbitration.

19. C: Option 2 is false; it should read that a panel will typically include a minority of arbitrators affiliated with securities industry.

20. D: An established account is one that has been open for at least one year.

21. B: Solicited transactions of penny stocks are always subject to the disclosure rules.

22. B: This information must be requested when opening a new account and RR must make a reasonable effort to obtain it. Additionally, this information is needed to comply with the Patriot Act, but it is not required information to open an account and transact business. Failure to obtain this information in a timely manner would likely cause the account to be frozen.

23. C: This is the only scenario where the RR would not need prior written authorization for discretionary trading.

24. B: Competency is the domain of the courts, not something granted by a power of attorney.

25. A: The other assets do not require the notifications and procedures of disclosure between member firms.

26. C: Minor's tax ID is used, and minor owns the asset on the trade date.

27. B: Volunteering for a 501c3 organization does not require notice or authorization. Arranging a loan and investing in a cattle venture would both be classified as private securities transactions and therefore require written notice regarding participation. A part-time job is considered an outside business activity and must have written notice as well.

28. B: Exceptions to the disclosure inclusion include radio broadcasts of 30 seconds or less, on electronic billboard signs, and on signs indicating location only. All other communications must contain these disclosures.

29. C: Complaint must be written, not just verbal. Any criminal offense other than a minor traffic violation must be reported. Expirations or non-renewals do not need to be reported, but denials of registration or expulsion would require prompt notice.

30. D: All of the above needs to be maintained for three years, not two.

31. B: All trade tickets must be retained for three years, not six.

32. D: All of the above. Participation is usually limited to specific entities as set forth under state law, or the rules of the particular LGIP.

33. False: 529 prepaid plans are not considered securities: they do not afford the donor any investment options, are not self-directed, and typically offer guaranteed returns.

34. D: These are some of the duties of a municipal securities principal.

35. D: Verbal authorization is not acceptable, it must be in writing.

36. False: MSRB considers disclosing only a current yield to be misleading. It considers the yield to maturity (YTM) or yield to call (YTC) to be the most important information. MSRB rules require that YTM or YTC be disclosed on customer confirmations.

37. D: All of the above are integral factors in determining the value of a call option.

38. C: The OCC does not have authority over approval of a firm's advertising, public communications or strategies.

39. B: Once assignment notice has been received the investor must accept the assignment. There are no possibilities of avoiding assignment once given.

40. D: Appropriateness when it comes to options can be somewhat subjective, but collars and puts are good ways to hedge away risk, while covered calls is a classic way to increase income without taking on additional risk. Uncovered put writing, however, brings more risk than income and would not be appropriate for someone interested in preservation of capital.

41. C: Selling a naked put is a good strategy when an investor wants to purchase stock at a lower price.

42. C: Long straddle is a strategy that will make money as long as there is volatility in the stock, regardless of whether the move is up or down.

43. B: A vertical spread is where the same options (calls or puts) are both bought and sold on the same security, with the same expiration date, but different strike prices. They are also called a price spread.

44. C: The net debit call spread and net credit put spread are both bullish strategies.

45. False: A butterfly spread is a strategy to make money on a stable stock price.

46. C: The CBOE does not use the S&P to determine what securities to provide LEAPS on and currently lists them on about 450 stocks as well as 10 indexes.

47. B: The VIX is designed to reflect expected stock market volatility over the next 30 days, not 60 days.

48. D: While it is true that banks do act as brokers for other banks and commercial clients on the Interbank Market, it is not true that they do not take positions for their own accounts.

49. True: Because the US dollar is the primary world reserve currency, it is always on one side of a foreign currency transaction.

50. A: There is no continuous ready market for FLEX Options. They are specialized—not standardized—contracts and therefore must go through a RFQ (request for quote) to create a market.

How to Overcome Test Anxiety

Just the thought of taking a test is enough to make most people a little nervous. A test is an important event that can have a long-term impact on your future, so it's important to take it seriously and it's natural to feel anxious about performing well. But just because anxiety is normal, that doesn't mean that it's helpful in test taking, or that you should simply accept it as part of your life. Anxiety can have a variety of effects. These effects can be mild, like making you feel slightly nervous, or severe, like blocking your ability to focus or remember even a simple detail.

If you experience test anxiety—whether severe or mild—it's important to know how to beat it. To discover this, first you need to understand what causes test anxiety.

Causes of Test Anxiety

While we often think of anxiety as an uncontrollable emotional state, it can actually be caused by simple, practical things. One of the most common causes of test anxiety is that a person does not feel adequately prepared for their test. This feeling can be the result of many different issues such as poor study habits or lack of organization, but the most common culprit is time management. Starting to study too late, failing to organize your study time to cover all of the material, or being distracted while you study will mean that you're not well prepared for the test. This may lead to cramming the night before, which will cause you to be physically and mentally exhausted for the test. Poor time management also contributes to feelings of stress, fear, and hopelessness as you realize you are not well prepared but don't know what to do about it.

Other times, test anxiety is not related to your preparation for the test but comes from unresolved fear. This may be a past failure on a test, or poor performance on tests in general. It may come from comparing yourself to others who seem to be performing better or from the stress of living up to expectations. Anxiety may be driven by fears of the future—how failure on this test would affect your educational and career goals. These fears are often completely irrational, but they can still negatively impact your test performance.

> **Review Video: <u>3 Reasons You Have Test Anxiety</u>**
> Visit mometrix.com/academy and enter code: 428468

Elements of Test Anxiety

As mentioned earlier, test anxiety is considered to be an emotional state, but it has physical and mental components as well. Sometimes you may not even realize that you are suffering from test anxiety until you notice the physical symptoms. These can include trembling hands, rapid heartbeat, sweating, nausea, and tense muscles. Extreme anxiety may lead to fainting or vomiting. Obviously, any of these symptoms can have a negative impact on testing. It is important to recognize them as soon as they begin to occur so that you can address the problem before it damages your performance.

> **Review Video: 3 Ways to Tell You Have Test Anxiety**
> Visit mometrix.com/academy and enter code: 927847

The mental components of test anxiety include trouble focusing and inability to remember learned information. During a test, your mind is on high alert, which can help you recall information and stay focused for an extended period of time. However, anxiety interferes with your mind's natural processes, causing you to blank out, even on the questions you know well. The strain of testing during anxiety makes it difficult to stay focused, especially on a test that may take several hours. Extreme anxiety can take a huge mental toll, making it difficult not only to recall test information but even to understand the test questions or pull your thoughts together.

> **Review Video: How Test Anxiety Affects Memory**
> Visit mometrix.com/academy and enter code: 609003

Effects of Test Anxiety

Test anxiety is like a disease—if left untreated, it will get progressively worse. Anxiety leads to poor performance, and this reinforces the feelings of fear and failure, which in turn lead to poor performances on subsequent tests. It can grow from a mild nervousness to a crippling condition. If allowed to progress, test anxiety can have a big impact on your schooling, and consequently on your future.

Test anxiety can spread to other parts of your life. Anxiety on tests can become anxiety in any stressful situation, and blanking on a test can turn into panicking in a job situation. But fortunately, you don't have to let anxiety rule your testing and determine your grades. There are a number of relatively simple steps you can take to move past anxiety and function normally on a test and in the rest of life.

> **Review Video: How Test Anxiety Impacts Your Grades**
> Visit mometrix.com/academy and enter code: 939819

Physical Steps for Beating Test Anxiety

While test anxiety is a serious problem, the good news is that it can be overcome. It doesn't have to control your ability to think and remember information. While it may take time, you can begin taking steps today to beat anxiety.

Just as your first hint that you may be struggling with anxiety comes from the physical symptoms, the first step to treating it is also physical. Rest is crucial for having a clear, strong mind. If you are tired, it is much easier to give in to anxiety. But if you establish good sleep habits, your body and mind will be ready to perform optimally, without the strain of exhaustion. Additionally, sleeping well helps you to retain information better, so you're more likely to recall the answers when you see the test questions.

Getting good sleep means more than going to bed on time. It's important to allow your brain time to relax. Take study breaks from time to time so it doesn't get overworked, and don't study right before bed. Take time to rest your mind before trying to rest your body, or you may find it difficult to fall asleep.

> **Review Video: The Importance of Sleep for Your Brain**
> Visit mometrix.com/academy and enter code: 319338

Along with sleep, other aspects of physical health are important in preparing for a test. Good nutrition is vital for good brain function. Sugary foods and drinks may give a burst of energy but this burst is followed by a crash, both physically and emotionally. Instead, fuel your body with protein and vitamin-rich foods.

Also, drink plenty of water. Dehydration can lead to headaches and exhaustion, especially if your brain is already under stress from the rigors of the test. Particularly if your test is a long one, drink water during the breaks. And if possible, take an energy-boosting snack to eat between sections.

> **Review Video: How Diet Can Affect your Mood**
> Visit mometrix.com/academy and enter code: 624317

Along with sleep and diet, a third important part of physical health is exercise. Maintaining a steady workout schedule is helpful, but even taking 5-minute study breaks to walk can help get your blood pumping faster and clear your head. Exercise also releases endorphins, which contribute to a positive feeling and can help combat test anxiety.

When you nurture your physical health, you are also contributing to your mental health. If your body is healthy, your mind is much more likely to be healthy as well. So take time to rest, nourish your body with healthy food and water, and get moving as much as possible. Taking these physical steps will make you stronger and more able to take the mental steps necessary to overcome test anxiety.

Copyright © Mometrix Media. You have been licensed one copy of this document for personal use only. Any other reproduction or redistribution is strictly prohibited. All rights reserved. This content is provided for test preparation purposes only and does not imply an endorsement by Mometrix of any particular political, scientific, or religious point of view.

Mental Steps for Beating Test Anxiety

Working on the mental side of test anxiety can be more challenging, but as with the physical side, there are clear steps you can take to overcome it. As mentioned earlier, test anxiety often stems from lack of preparation, so the obvious solution is to prepare for the test. Effective studying may be the most important weapon you have for beating test anxiety, but you can and should employ several other mental tools to combat fear.

First, boost your confidence by reminding yourself of past success—tests or projects that you aced. If you're putting as much effort into preparing for this test as you did for those, there's no reason you should expect to fail here. Work hard to prepare; then trust your preparation.

Second, surround yourself with encouraging people. It can be helpful to find a study group, but be sure that the people you're around will encourage a positive attitude. If you spend time with others who are anxious or cynical, this will only contribute to your own anxiety. Look for others who are motivated to study hard from a desire to succeed, not from a fear of failure.

Third, reward yourself. A test is physically and mentally tiring, even without anxiety, and it can be helpful to have something to look forward to. Plan an activity following the test, regardless of the outcome, such as going to a movie or getting ice cream.

When you are taking the test, if you find yourself beginning to feel anxious, remind yourself that you know the material. Visualize successfully completing the test. Then take a few deep, relaxing breaths and return to it. Work through the questions carefully but with confidence, knowing that you are capable of succeeding.

Developing a healthy mental approach to test taking will also aid in other areas of life. Test anxiety affects more than just the actual test—it can be damaging to your mental health and even contribute to depression. It's important to beat test anxiety before it becomes a problem for more than testing.

Review Video: <u>Test Anxiety and Depression</u>
Visit mometrix.com/academy and enter code: 904704

Study Strategy

Being prepared for the test is necessary to combat anxiety, but what does being prepared look like? You may study for hours on end and still not feel prepared. What you need is a strategy for test prep. The next few pages outline our recommended steps to help you plan out and conquer the challenge of preparation.

STEP 1: SCOPE OUT THE TEST

Learn everything you can about the format (multiple choice, essay, etc.) and what will be on the test. Gather any study materials, course outlines, or sample exams that may be available. Not only will this help you to prepare, but knowing what to expect can help to alleviate test anxiety.

STEP 2: MAP OUT THE MATERIAL

Look through the textbook or study guide and make note of how many chapters or sections it has. Then divide these over the time you have. For example, if a book has 15 chapters and you have five days to study, you need to cover three chapters each day. Even better, if you have the time, leave an extra day at the end for overall review after you have gone through the material in depth.

If time is limited, you may need to prioritize the material. Look through it and make note of which sections you think you already have a good grasp on, and which need review. While you are studying, skim quickly through the familiar sections and take more time on the challenging parts. Write out your plan so you don't get lost as you go. Having a written plan also helps you feel more in control of the study, so anxiety is less likely to arise from feeling overwhelmed at the amount to cover.

STEP 3: GATHER YOUR TOOLS

Decide what study method works best for you. Do you prefer to highlight in the book as you study and then go back over the highlighted portions? Or do you type out notes of the important information? Or is it helpful to make flashcards that you can carry with you? Assemble the pens, index cards, highlighters, post-it notes, and any other materials you may need so you won't be distracted by getting up to find things while you study.

If you're having a hard time retaining the information or organizing your notes, experiment with different methods. For example, try color-coding by subject with colored pens, highlighters, or post-it notes. If you learn better by hearing, try recording yourself reading your notes so you can listen while in the car, working out, or simply sitting at your desk. Ask a friend to quiz you from your flashcards, or try teaching someone the material to solidify it in your mind.

STEP 4: CREATE YOUR ENVIRONMENT

It's important to avoid distractions while you study. This includes both the obvious distractions like visitors and the subtle distractions like an uncomfortable chair (or a too-comfortable couch that makes you want to fall asleep). Set up the best study environment possible: good lighting and a comfortable work area. If background music helps you focus, you may want to turn it on, but otherwise keep the room quiet. If you are using a computer to take notes, be sure you don't have any other windows open, especially applications like social media, games, or anything else that could distract you. Silence your phone and turn off notifications. Be sure to keep water close by so you stay hydrated while you study (but avoid unhealthy drinks and snacks).

Also, take into account the best time of day to study. Are you freshest first thing in the morning? Try to set aside some time then to work through the material. Is your mind clearer in the afternoon or evening? Schedule your study session then. Another method is to study at the same time of day that you will take the test, so that your brain gets used to working on the material at that time and will be ready to focus at test time.

STEP 5: STUDY!

Once you have done all the study preparation, it's time to settle into the actual studying. Sit down, take a few moments to settle your mind so you can focus, and begin to follow your study plan. Don't give in to distractions or let yourself procrastinate. This is your time to prepare so you'll be ready to fearlessly approach the test. Make the most of the time and stay focused.

Of course, you don't want to burn out. If you study too long you may find that you're not retaining the information very well. Take regular study breaks. For example, taking five minutes out of every hour to walk briskly, breathing deeply and swinging your arms, can help your mind stay fresh.

As you get to the end of each chapter or section, it's a good idea to do a quick review. Remind yourself of what you learned and work on any difficult parts. When you feel that you've mastered the material, move on to the next part. At the end of your study session, briefly skim through your notes again.

But while review is helpful, cramming last minute is NOT. If at all possible, work ahead so that you won't need to fit all your study into the last day. Cramming overloads your brain with more information than it can process and retain, and your tired mind may struggle to recall even previously learned information when it is overwhelmed with last-minute study. Also, the urgent nature of cramming and the stress placed on your brain contribute to anxiety. You'll be more likely to go to the test feeling unprepared and having trouble thinking clearly.

So don't cram, and don't stay up late before the test, even just to review your notes at a leisurely pace. Your brain needs rest more than it needs to go over the information again. In fact, plan to finish your studies by noon or early afternoon the day before the test. Give your brain the rest of the day to relax or focus on other things, and get a good night's sleep. Then you will be fresh for the test and better able to recall what you've studied.

STEP 6: TAKE A PRACTICE TEST

Many courses offer sample tests, either online or in the study materials. This is an excellent resource to check whether you have mastered the material, as well as to prepare for the test format and environment.

Check the test format ahead of time: the number of questions, the type (multiple choice, free response, etc.), and the time limit. Then create a plan for working through them. For example, if you have 30 minutes to take a 60-question test, your limit is 30 seconds per question. Spend less time on the questions you know well so that you can take more time on the difficult ones.

If you have time to take several practice tests, take the first one open book, with no time limit. Work through the questions at your own pace and make sure you fully understand them. Gradually work up to taking a test under test conditions: sit at a desk with all study materials put away and set a timer. Pace yourself to make sure you finish the test with time to spare and go back to check your answers if you have time.

After each test, check your answers. On the questions you missed, be sure you understand why you missed them. Did you misread the question (tests can use tricky wording)? Did you forget the information? Or was it something you hadn't learned? Go back and study any shaky areas that the practice tests reveal.

Taking these tests not only helps with your grade, but also aids in combating test anxiety. If you're already used to the test conditions, you're less likely to worry about it, and working through tests until you're scoring well gives you a confidence boost. Go through the practice tests until you feel comfortable, and then you can go into the test knowing that you're ready for it.

Test Tips

On test day, you should be confident, knowing that you've prepared well and are ready to answer the questions. But aside from preparation, there are several test day strategies you can employ to maximize your performance.

First, as stated before, get a good night's sleep the night before the test (and for several nights before that, if possible). Go into the test with a fresh, alert mind rather than staying up late to study.

Try not to change too much about your normal routine on the day of the test. It's important to eat a nutritious breakfast, but if you normally don't eat breakfast at all, consider eating just a protein bar. If you're a coffee drinker, go ahead and have your normal coffee. Just make sure you time it so that the caffeine doesn't wear off right in the middle of your test. Avoid sugary beverages, and drink enough water to stay hydrated but not so much that you need a restroom break 10 minutes into the test. If your test isn't first thing in the morning, consider going for a walk or doing a light workout before the test to get your blood flowing.

Allow yourself enough time to get ready, and leave for the test with plenty of time to spare so you won't have the anxiety of scrambling to arrive in time. Another reason to be early is to select a good seat. It's helpful to sit away from doors and windows, which can be distracting. Find a good seat, get out your supplies, and settle your mind before the test begins.

When the test begins, start by going over the instructions carefully, even if you already know what to expect. Make sure you avoid any careless mistakes by following the directions.

Then begin working through the questions, pacing yourself as you've practiced. If you're not sure on an answer, don't spend too much time on it, and don't let it shake your confidence. Either skip it and come back later, or eliminate as many wrong answers as possible and guess among the remaining ones. Don't dwell on these questions as you continue—put them out of your mind and focus on what lies ahead.

Be sure to read all of the answer choices, even if you're sure the first one is the right answer. Sometimes you'll find a better one if you keep reading. But don't second-guess yourself if you do immediately know the answer. Your gut instinct is usually right. Don't let test anxiety rob you of the information you know.

If you have time at the end of the test (and if the test format allows), go back and review your answers. Be cautious about changing any, since your first instinct tends to be correct, but make sure you didn't misread any of the questions or accidentally mark the wrong answer choice. Look over any you skipped and make an educated guess.

At the end, leave the test feeling confident. You've done your best, so don't waste time worrying about your performance or wishing you could change anything. Instead, celebrate the successful completion of this test. And finally, use this test to learn how to deal with anxiety even better next time.

> **Review Video: 5 Tips to Beat Test Anxiety**
> Visit mometrix.com/academy and enter code: 570656

Important Qualification

Not all anxiety is created equal. If your test anxiety is causing major issues in your life beyond the classroom or testing center, or if you are experiencing troubling physical symptoms related to your anxiety, it may be a sign of a serious physiological or psychological condition. If this sounds like your situation, we strongly encourage you to seek professional help.

Thank You

We at Mometrix would like to extend our heartfelt thanks to you, our friend and patron, for allowing us to play a part in your journey. It is a privilege to serve people from all walks of life who are unified in their commitment to building the best future they can for themselves.

The preparation you devote to these important testing milestones may be the most valuable educational opportunity you have for making a real difference in your life. We encourage you to put your heart into it—that feeling of succeeding, overcoming, and yes, conquering will be well worth the hours you've invested.

We want to hear your story, your struggles and your successes, and if you see any opportunities for us to improve our materials so we can help others even more effectively in the future, please share that with us as well. **The team at Mometrix would be absolutely thrilled to hear from you!** So please, send us an email (support@mometrix.com) and let's stay in touch.

> **If you'd like some additional help, check out these other resources we offer for your exam:**
> **http://MometrixFlashcards.com/Series910**

Additional Bonus Material

Due to our efforts to try to keep this book to a manageable length, we've created a link that will give you access to all of your additional bonus material:

mometrix.com/bonus948/series910